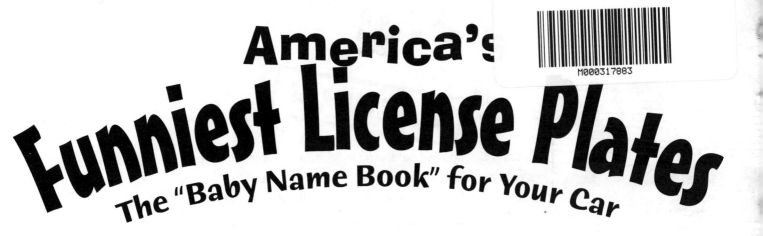

America's Funniest License Plates

The "Baby Name Book" for Your Car

BY TED FORD

Many of the plates shown in this book may be available in your state!

WARNING!

Reading this book while driving may cause brain cramp, eye strain, motion sickness, dizziness, irreparable harm to your vehicle, and sharply increased auto insurance premiums!

ISBN: 0-9664447-6-0

If you are interested in purchasing copies of this book or a customized version of it for fundraising or promotional purposes, contact the author for information about wholesale pricing:

Ted Ford
ted@licenseplatefun.com

Foreword

Anybody who tells you they don't read personalized license plates would probably lie about other stuff too. There are three kinds of drivers: those who have personalized plates, those who read them, and those who think all the good ones are already taken. I have good news for those of you in the last category. This book is proof that even with 10 million personalized plates in America, there's still a limitless supply of great ideas. Just when I think I've seen everything, I'll spot a plate that makes me laugh so hard that the driver behind me thinks I flunked drivers' ed.

Back in the late 1980s I was following a black Porsche Carrera on the 405 freeway near Los Angeles with a plate that read PONOMO . Traffic was bumper to bumper, so I pulled up alongside and asked the driver, who looked like a Lakers player, what his plate meant. It was so funny the way he said, "Well, I used to be po', but I ain't po' no mo'!"

That did it for me. I wanted a cool plate too. But like most car owners, I couldn't come up with the right idea. I scoured libraries and bookstores, looking for a "baby name book" for cars, and was shocked to learn that no such book existed. So, two years later, after researching three million personalized plates from DMV lists,

I published my first book of plate ideas, *California Traffic Talk*, which quickly sold out.

But my passion to create a book to help motorists like myself come up with the perfect plate was not satisfied. I wanted to produce one that would entertain readers while giving them creative ideas. You hold in your hands the result. *America's Funniest License Plates* brings together the creativity of hundreds of the most outgoing, enthusiastic, successful, and—above all—humorous people you'd ever hope to meet.

Behind every creative plate is a story. I can't count how many red lights I've run, how many illegal U-turns I've made, and how many total strangers I have approached to get the story. In addition to the photos of plates and their owners, I have included my own plate ideas that I have developed over the years. Many are still available in your state.

If you start noticing creative license plates more than ever after reading this book, just thank "Mr. PONOMO" on the 405!

Contents

Everyone Loves
Personalized ~~Plates~~
creative!

Reading personalized license plates is a national pastime. Every day I meet people who tell me they're always looking for personalized plates while they're behind the wheel.

Driving around with a creative plate tells people a lot about you. Before they ever meet you, they know you are fun, witty, and creative. They are naturally inclined to like you. A creative license plate is a great conversation starter, whether you're looking for a date, trying to drum up business, or just want to express your individuality.

Never underestimate the importance of first impressions. In the world of business, they often make or break the sale. That's why, for example, the infomercials that I produce for all sorts of companies are so successful. These little four-to-five-minute video presentations that can be viewed on DVD or on a company's web site are carefully scripted to introduce the company in the most favorable light, so that the prospect comes away thinking they would be a fool to go with anyone else.

Scott Bailey (page 10) is a good example of a driver who uses his license plate to make a good first impression. Not only does he have a very nice Porsche Carrera, but I learned that he is an energetic, successful elementary school principal who gives motivational instruction to other school principals throughout the country. Before you even meet him, his plate tells you that he's a go-getter with a sense of humor. If it weren't for his plate, you probably would never have met him. Neither would I.

You Have a Choice

Let's face it. Every license plate is personalized. The question is, who is going to choose what your license plate says—you, or the DMV? See for yourself the dramatic difference between what they will give you, and what you can come up with for yourself.

Please circle the correct answer.

Here we have two BMWs. One has a license plate that tells you the owner has a high degree of creativity, a great sense of humor, and is a good sport in traffic. Can you guess which one? (Like, duh!)

Warning! Plates Rated by OPRA

The OPRA Rating System

The photographed plates shown in this book have been rated for humor and approved by the Official Plate Rating Association (OPRA) of America. The OPRA team was very carefully hand picked by the author (his advisory board were left totally out of any decision making process).

Great! Pretty good So-so Sucks Really sucks

Indecent Exposure

Cars this nice should not be exposed to the public without a personalized plate. There "auto" be a name for this sort of abuse. I mean, these poor cars are practically naked!

A Mini Cooper whimpers in the parking lot, "Gimme, gimme! I need, I need!"

Maybe the name of the owner of this beautiful Porsche Carrera is 638 MAR.

Cars That Beg for Personalized Plates

Some car makes just have to have a personalized license plate. The vehicle is simply not complete without it. Your choice of car says a lot about you. After all, you are what you drive! Make sure the statement is complete with just the right creative plate. Some automobiles are so classy, so cool, so fun, or so over the top that a personalized license plate should be standard equipment. Look over the examples on the following pages and see what I mean!

The author demonstrates a simple, sure-fire method to transform a run-of-the-mill luxury car into one that will get noticed.

AUTOS

Porsche, of Course!

As a Porsche owner, you owe it to your audience in traffic to have a creative plate. Don't disappoint them.

Is there any other way?

You can bet Scott Bailey, principal at Wayne Tanaka Elementary in Las Vegas, is never late to school! Click on his link at www.licenseplatefun.com to find out about his seminars for educators.

Short and sweet. The owner of this Porsche Boxter likes everything just "so."

Did you know that | PORSCHE | correctly spelled with all seven letters can only be put on the license plate of one vehicle in each state?

True Porsche Story:

A Porsche owner in California owned the correctly spelled Porsche (| PORSCHE |) license plate. Another Porsche owner wanted the plate badly enough that he paid the owner of the plate $5,000 for it!

A 911 will do.

A911LDO

FASPRSH

911 LDO

POR ME

POORSHA

POOR ME

Jag Tags

Driving a Jaquar without a creative tag is like walking around in public in your undies.

What is it with Jaguar owners? Do they get frisky after 40?

Now, **these** Jaguar owners understand their civic duty
to display an entertaining plate!

That's right. That's what it's all about.

AUTOS

Mercedes Mania

A Mercedes says class. A standard-issue plate doesn't.

Tom & Carol Peterson of MountainCork.com sporting goods love to play, and it shows.

You wondered how they found Saddam Hussein in that rat hole? The plate on the Mercedes sitting outside tipped them off.

AUTOS

Kim Buchanan is a well-to-do industrial contractor. His fifteen-year-old son, Skyler, is into hockey in a big way. They both share a love for flashy vehicles and equally flashy license plates. Kim's Hummer H2 is on page 49.

Like Father, Like Son

Skyler declares his first love on his very own 4×4.

If Kim's '04 Dodge Viper doesn't catch your attention, his plate ("snake bit") certainly will!

Skyler poses with his father's "US Made" Harley and his own "Skywalker" Harley.

The Making of a Great Plate

I have met a lot of awesome people in the course of putting this book together. One of them is Preston James Christensen, the owner of a red Dodge Viper that sports the plate WIFE OK'D. The instant I saw his plate as he passed me in a parking lot, I knew he needed to be in this book! A quick U-turn, a handshake, and a Jamba Juice later, I had made a new friend.

Before I even met Preston, his license plate told me four things about him: (1) He's married; (2) he has a great sense of humor; (3) he was clever enough not only to be able to afford a car like that, but to talk his wife into letting him get it; and (4)

he's definitely an innovative thinker.

Preston tells how he came up with his fantastic plate:

"There were several things I was thinking about while trying to come up with what my first personalized license plate would say. Whatever it said, I wanted it to be instantly readable, and something where you didn't have to sit there all day thinking about it. I also wanted it to be funny to everyone (not just funny to me). My wife had told me for years she wouldn't approve of a car like that until absolutely everything else (financially speaking) was taken care of—so I wanted to work that in. And finally, I knew I only had 7 spaces (letters and numbers) to work with!"

What has the reaction been to Preston's plate?

"It makes cruising around town in a Viper all the more fun!" says Preston. "There's hardly a car I catch in the rear view mirror where the driver isn't busting up laughing. I've seen people sit up,

16

stop conversations, point—and just have a lot of fun with it. If a silly license plate can make an entire family in a camper laugh, or de-stress someone after a crappy day, or maybe just lighten the mood, well, isn't that what it's all about?"

So what did Preston do to convince his wife to go along with his dream car? He explains, "When I was 29 years old, in 1998, I'd had a lot of different jobs, and wasn't real happy with what I was doing. And on the side, I had always been very interested in, yet very frustrated with, investing my money, particularly in the stock market."

To make a long story short, he finally took the "bull by the horns," as they say, and started to get some real answers. "I figured if I wanted good results, I'd better find out from successful people what to do, so I literally started calling up famous authors and successful investors I'd seen in magazines and

Preston James Christensen ("The Pirate") with his wife Melissa, his children Collin, Will, and Leah, and his "wife OK'd" Viper

on TV. I'd call them right up on the phone, pretending I was a big shot myself, and interviewed them and took lots of notes."

The result was his own very successful website for investors (www.bullbythehorns.com) and a daily newsletter subscription that reaches thousands of investors.

"I found my true passion in teaching others about a subject I truly love. I help true beginners along, as well as teach stock trading strategies to more seasoned investors. And along the way, I picked up the nickname 'Pirate' as I help investors uncover the 'buried treasure' and show them where the profits are really hiding on Wall Street!"

Visit
www.bullbythehorns.com
and discover what Preston
can do for you!

Beemer Me Up, Scotty!

BMW stands for Bavarian Motor Works, not "Boring Motor Vehicle." Your tag should make that clear.

A sunny plate will keep this yellow BMW warm all winter long.

Wait a minute — something's wrong with this picture!

Other alternatives would be:

NMPLOYD NMPLOID

Our bet is, these guys are partners in an employment agency. (Only their BMW salesman knows for sure ...)

AUTOS

'Til 2012 ?

Marketing pro Richard Ostler says his wife lets him have a new Beemer only once every fifteen years. He only has to wait until 2012 for the next one!

The Ultimate Accessory for Your Car

So, you have the perfect car with all the options—the sun roof, the stereo CD with XM Radio, the hands-free cell phone and GPS navigating system, even the fuzzy dice. But did you remember the most important accessory of all—the one that every motorist will see as you cruise by them? Auto manufacturers invest millions of dollars and years of work designing every feature of the cars they sell. Shouldn't you at least put a bit of thought and effort into the one feature that sets your car apart from every other car of the same model—that little 6" x 12" piece of tin on the back that is uniquely yours? Think of a clever vanity plate as the ultimate accessory to set your car apart from all the rest!

These kids have the right idea on how to make their "tricked out" car complete!

Wild Mustangs

Kickin' up its heels and rarin' to go, the Ford Mustang is a natural when it comes to inspiring creative plate ideas. Check out the ideas on these two pages. Several are probably still available in your state!

AUTOS

MUSTANG

MESTANG

the 'Stang — THESTNG

fast 'Stang — FASTANG

the 'Stang — STANGME

THSTANG

horseplay — HORSPLA

SADDLUP

RIDE ME

MUSTHAV

RYD THIS

MYSTANG

SUM RIDE

IT BUCKS

IT BUX

LASSOME

BUCKROO

WHOA UP

WO PONY

BADPONY

RUFRIDE

BADRIDE

rough rider — RUFRIDR

rough rider — WOHORSY

RUFRYDR

BUXSKIN

MY STUD

WILDPNY

wild pony — STUD 4U

YLDPONY

wild child — RARN2GO

WILCHLD

wild child — GIDDYUP

YLDCHLD

horse pucky — HORSPKY

PONY UP

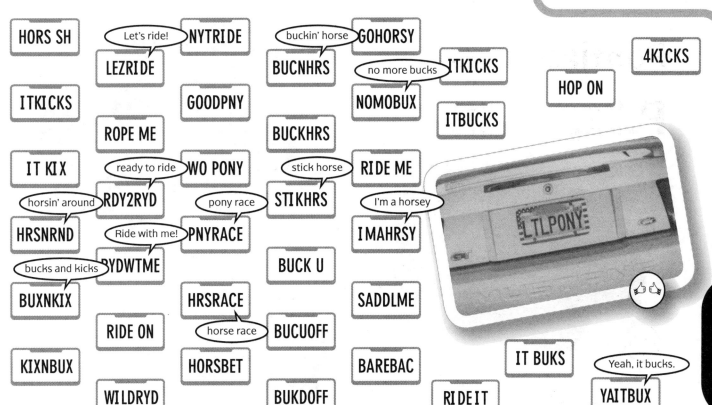

HORS SH

Let's ride!

NYTRIDE

LEZRIDE

buckin' horse

GOHORSY

BUCNHRS

no more bucks

ITKICKS

4KICKS

NOMOBUX

HOP ON

ITKICKS

GOODPNY

ITBUCKS

ROPE ME

BUCKHRS

IT KIX

ready to ride

WO PONY

stick horse

RIDE ME

RDY2RYD

STIKHRS

horsin' around

pony race

I'm a horsey

HRSNRND

PNYRACE

IMAHRSY

Ride with me!

BYDWTME

BUCK U

bucks and kicks

BUXNKIX

HRSRACE

SADDLME

RIDE ON

horse race

BUCUOFF

IT BUKS

Yeah, it bucks.

KIXNBUX

HORSBET

BAREBAC

YAITBUX

WILDRYD

BUKDOFF

RIDEIT

LTLPONY

AUTOS

Pontiac Fever

Pontiac's muscle cars—Trans Ams, etc.—scream for attention and a personalized plate.

But where'd you go? We'll need a full explanation; please write us...

Too bad the speed limit is 25!

Well, **excuuuse you!**

AUTOS

What's worth it? The car — or the driver?

Idea man and entrepreneur Paul Stoddard says his classic Trans Am is quicker than WHAT?

AUTOS

Pet 'Vettes

If your "pet" is a Chevy Corvette, it's just plain sick if you let it run around without a custom tag.

Dr. Derek Maclean, a Las Vegas dentist, likes the way his new Corvette handles. (Ain't it smooth?)

Gee, Erica, I bought this nice, red 'Vette because I love you so much. Oh, that license plate? It's to remind all the guys who I bought it for.

AUTOS

MIXED SIGNALS?

You asked for it, you got it. Nice 'Vette!

Is this "mixed signs," as in signals, or is the name of your business MX Signs? (Our editing staff needs an explanation.)

AUTOS

Sexy Lexus

If you can afford a Lexus, you can afford a creative plate. Here are some Lexus-themed plate ideas. Some may still be available in your state.

Although there's nothing **creative** about this plate, it is **unique**. Only 50 people in the United States can have a plate that says this — one in each state.

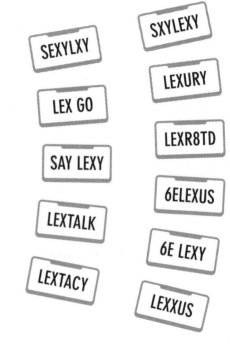

SEXYLXY

SXYLEXY

LEX GO

LEXURY

SAY LEXY

LEXR8TD

LEXTALK

6ELEXUS

LEXTACY

6E LEXY

LEXXUS

AUTOS

What do you want to bet we're following a marathon runner?

Lynn Fairbanks, retired top sales executive for O.C. Tanner jewelry company, will always find a way.

AUTOS

Audis and Innies

| NOT A VW | LKYAUDI |

Regardless of whether you have an "outie" or an "innie," if you drive an Audi, you're in the "in" crowd. Say it with pride with a creative license plate. On this and the following page are forty specifically Audi-themed plates, many of which may still be available in your state.

Ruth Norton says her TT Turbo is total fun.

| AUDICAR |
| NR AUDI |
| UCNOWDY |
| HOTAUDI |
| SXYAUDI |
| OSMAUDI |

yup, sure 'nuf: They're driving a TT Turbo.

| SUMAUDI |
| SUMOWDI |
| ANYAUDI |
| OWDYINY |
| AUDI NE |

| AUDIANY | OWDINNY | AUDI 4X |

AUTOS

OW DEE	AUDI DO	AUDIYAL
OWDEEEE	OWDI DO	AUDIUAL
HOW DEE	AUDIDEW	AUDIYOL
SAYAUDI	OWDYDEW	AUDIACE
SAHOWDI	OWDOUDO	AUDIOSE
SAHAUDI	AUDIBLE	AUDIOZE
OWDIOSE	AUDIBUL	OWDYOSE
NAUDI	AUDIROX	OWDYOZE

What a Gomer!

AUTOS

The Mini Series

The Mini Cooper is so small that a license plate takes up a lot of real estate on the back of the car—which means your message will stand out all the more! See how Mini drivers are capitalizing on the benefits of thinking small.

Jan Evans never has trouble finding her Mini Cooper in the parking lot.

TRUE CONFESSION

New Mini owner Phillip Bandley racks his brain to think of a personalized plate! Can you feel his pain?

AUTOS

If at first you don't succeed at spelling "cooper," try, try again!

Let's motor!

Nice play on Mini's slogan.

— signed, Mickey!
(Ain't that cute?)

AUTOS

Joe and Kathy Mardasich replaced their Chevy Suburban with "his" and "hers" Mini Coopers.

Up Close and Personalized

I was cruising southbound on the interstate. Up ahead I see a red Porsche Boxter convertible. I kind of ease up behind it to see what the plate says.

The driver spots me in his rear-view mirror. I'm being dissed because I'm only in a white Ford Explorer (no fancy trim; definitely not an Eddie Bauer edition). He's feelin' superior in his freshly washed Porsche with a Zaino Brothers shine and Armorall on the tires.

Then I finally see the license plate. Not what you would expect at all. Just a boring, standard piece of rectangular tin—a piece of nothin'. It read 1703N. That's it. 1703N. I even tried to see if that could mean something. Nope. Just 1703N. What a dud.

The moral of this story: No matter where you go in traffic, someone is always checking out your rear end. So make sure when they get "up close and personal," your booty's worth lookin' at!

37

Jus' Cruisin'

Some vehicles get more attention in traffic than others. The P.T. Cruiser is a good example. Its compact size helps to show off a creative plate.

No, this PT Cruiser ain't **part** mine. It's **all** mine. Mine! All mine!

A creative Cruiser driver. They're not ashamed!

AUTOS

VWs, Bugs, and Other Critters

What make of car is the favorite of creative plate owners? Hands down, it has to be the Volkswagen "bug." VW owners, like drunk drivers, prove that you don't have to spend a lot of money to get noticed in traffic!

Do I bug you?

DUIBUGU

HERBIE1

680,000 new VW's and we finally found HERBIE! He lives!

LADYBUG

WHEE W

UBUGME

BUGPUKY

AUTOS

AUTOS

BUGHUNT

Stu Naisbitt, shown here with his VW, told me his family also has `PLN NUTS` and `CMDU26.2` ("see'm do 26.2" — as in marathons). Very clever, Stu!

Yessir, Al Thomas is the proud owner of this classic '67 convertible VW. Just don't mention Christmas!

BUGNYOU

Am I buggin' you?

MIBUGNU

gone buggy

GONBGGY

Here I am, caught red-handed, collecting a specimen.

bug eyes for you

BUGII4U

Dee's dreams have come true. She got the car, the plate, and her 15 minutes of fame.

AUTOS

VOLKSWAGEN

BUG OUT

beetle mania

BTLMNIA

BUGBUNY

Oh, valet parker man ... that's my Bug ... yes, the **unique** one!

BUGOLA

UNIOBUG

Elementary school teacher Jan Blair won't take any crapola in her classroom, but she'll take her "bugola" most anywhere!

BUGSY'S

IMA VW

WABBIT

SQUISH

Bugsy's

BUG ZZ

AUTOS

BUGGAUF

WWW.VW

BUG OFF

CUTEASA

ALLR·NUN

SNAPS
INTERMOUNTAIN

B TULL

This plate works
for both the car
and the owner.

Are we following some
"all-or-nothing" types,
or this is the "sister mobile"
from the local nunnery?

What do you know . . .
A snapping beetle!

AUTOS

The Story of the Three Little Bugs

Once upon a time there were three little bugs:

Papa bug ...   Mama bug ...   and little baby boring bug ...

... who couldn't think of nuthin'!

olks are drawn to Jeeps and personalized license plates for the same reason — to have fun!

Jeepers, Creepers!

... and I always thought it was "**G WIZ**"!

Karen Webb confesses that this name just seemed to flow naturally.

AUTOS

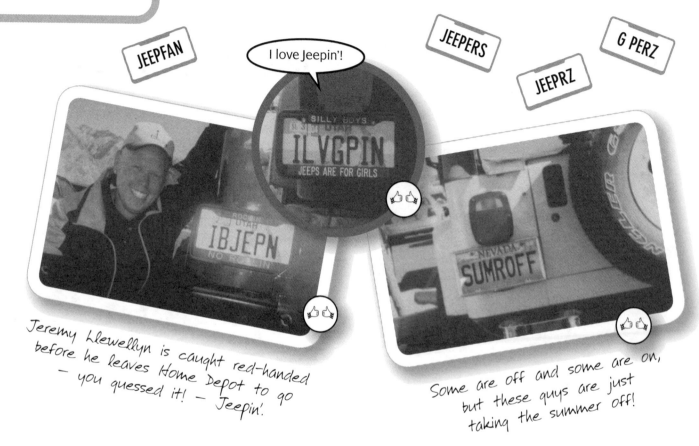

AUTOS

Jeremy Llewellyn is caught red-handed before he leaves Home Depot to go — you guessed it! — Jeepin'.

Some are off and some are on, but these guys are just taking the summer off!

"Moody" or "muddy" — either way it gets your attention. (Maybe it depends on the day.)

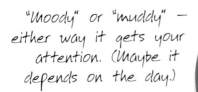

Staci Lea told us her dad thought her **bright** yellow Jeep was obnoxious. Heck, it gave her a great idea, huh?

Behind every personalized plate is a story. Camille Cannon and her husband Rex own several self-serve car washes. No need to put "WASH ME" on her back window!

AUTOS

Quick: Which two license plates reveal that their owners are creative, have a great sense of humor, had an extra $55, and aren't afraid to be noticed?

You've Heard of the Three Tenors?

Now meet the three Hummers . . .

MMMM·V

XSINGER

I'm thinkin' about it . . .

HMMMMMM

can't sing

CNTSING

can't sing

CANTSNG

NO WORDS

HMNALNG

H2 OH

Kim Buchanan obviously loves water, Harleys, and his Hummer H2.

Dan Todd is just "hummin'" along.

AUTOS

How to Get Noticed in Traffic

Warren Jones (right) has it all figured out: (1) buy a humongous Hummer; (2) get it tricked out to the max; and then, as the finishing touch, (3) add a clever plate. Works every time. (Check out the handiwork of Jeremy Manning, who souped up Warren's Hummer! If you'd like to see about having your vehicle modified like this, click on Jeremy's link at **www.licenseplatefun.com**.)

Warren Jones drives one hummer of a Hummer!

Oldies But Goodies

Vintage autos always turn heads.
Their plates should too!

A REAL CLASSIC!

Ernest Muirhead poses by his 1914 Model T Ford.

Quick! What do Jackie Rodgers and her 450 SL Mercedes have in common? They're both classics!

Toyotas Are TOYRIFK !

Not only are Toyotas great cars, the name just begs to be played with!

TOYODA

MY TOY

BOY TOY

toy-riffic
TOYRIFC

GOTATOY

LITLTOY

toy truck
TOYTWUK

NUFTOYS

ANEWTOY

enough toys

toyin' 'round
TOYNRND

TOYSTRY

TOYSTOR

toy story

TOYRIFK

toyin' with you

jus' toyin'
JUSTOYN

TOYZRME

TOY CAR

TOYNWTU

TOYSRME

TOYSRUS

NEWTOYZ

GOTTOYS

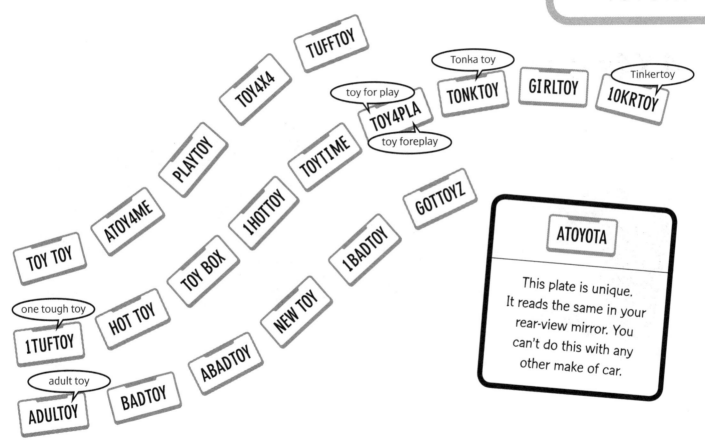

TUFFTOY

TOY4X4

Tonka toy
TONKTOY

GIRLTOY

Tinkertoy
10KRTOY

toy for play
TOY4PLA

toy foreplay

PLAYTOY

TOYTIME

ATOY4ME

1HOTTOY

GOTTOYZ

TOY TOY

TOY BOX

1BADTOY

one tough toy
1TUFTOY

HOT TOY

NEW TOY

ABADTOY

adult toy
ADULTOY

BADTOY

ATOYOTA

This plate is unique.
It reads the same in your
rear-view mirror. You
can't do this with any
other make of car.

AUTOS

4X4s 4 U

SUVs and 4X4s are favorites of fun-loving people. No wonder you see so many creative plates on the tail of these vehicles.

Proving once again that great minds think the same — even in different states!

AUTOS

4X4NITE	SOME 4X			
FORDBY4	BAD BY4	FUN2 4X		
4D BY 4	BAD X4	GOT 4X		

ROV·N·RND

GONE4XN	4SOME	4XROCKS		
GO SUVN	AJEEPUV	R8TDWLD *(rated wild)*	SUV BMW	TLKDRTY
NSUV UC *(an SUV, you see)*	R8TDSUV *(rated SUV)*	R8TDYLD *(rated wild)*	ESS UV	GETDRTY
SUVR8TD *(SUV rated)*	UCN SUV *(You see an SUV.)*	SUVZGR8 *(SUV's great.)*	SUV 4ME	WOWNSUV *(Wow, an SUV!)*
GOT SUV	TOY SUV	1GR8SUV *(one great SUV)*	NMY SUV *(in my SUV)*	SUVTHIS
GOTNSUV	SUV 2C	AWSMSUV *(awesome SUV)*	THSMSUV *(this some SUV)*	HOT SUV
NEEDSUV	FORDXUV	OSM SUV *(awesome SUV)*	123 SUV	UGOT4X4
IMN SUV *(I am an SUV.)*	OBOYSUV	R8TDFUN *(rated fun)*	SUV VW	BAD 4X

IT ROX	ROCKMY4	QWIK 4X
4BY44U	4X4 FUN	WEGO4XN
1TUF4X4	4XFOLKS	WEGO 4X

SUVs & 4X4s

Four-by-four tonight
4X42NYT

Four-by-in' to the max
4XN2DMX

Four-by-in' rocks!
4XNROX

4X2NITE

on all fours
ONAL4RS

cool four-by
KQQL 4X

4 MUD 4

4XSEEYA

on all fours
ONALL4Z

cool four-by-er
KQQL4XR

4 MUD X

way-high four-by
WAHI4X

way up high
WAYUPHI

4BYBY4

4X44MUD

four-by see ya
4X CYA

HI4XHUH

4BYE4

GOT DIRT

4X BYBY

SOME4X4

Yay! Let's four-by!
YALEZ4X

4 DIRT X

I'll four-by ya
IL4X YA

four-by-Ford
4X4 4RD

GOT MUD

1 BAD 4X

a way-high four-by
AWAHI4X

SUM 4X4

for the mud
4DUHMUD

DO U 4X

SCARY4X

4BYE44U

muddy boy
MUDYBOY

BABY4X4

4X GONE

There's no mistakin' that this is a Ford 4 X 4.

4X2DAY

THS4X4U
This 4X4 [is] for you.

DIRTHVN

ILL4XYA

SEKC 4X
sexy four-by

4BFREND

DRTHEVN
dirt heaven

4BOY4

LEZGO4X
Let's go four-by!

4XFRENZ
four-by friends

TOOLIES

UGLY 4X

GONE4XN

4XFRNZY
four-by frenzy

4D2LEZ
for the toolies

SEXY 4X

GON4BYN

LQQKN4X
lookin' four-by

WAKO4X4
wacko 4X4

IL 4XU

4XWHAT

4XLQQK

KRZY 4X

AWSM4X4
awesome 4X4

WHOZ4X

4X GONE

HOT2 4X

10SM4X4
one awesome 4X4

FOUR X 4

WHATMUD

LETS 4X

WAOSM4X
way awesome 4X4

A Ford Explorer owner gets cute.

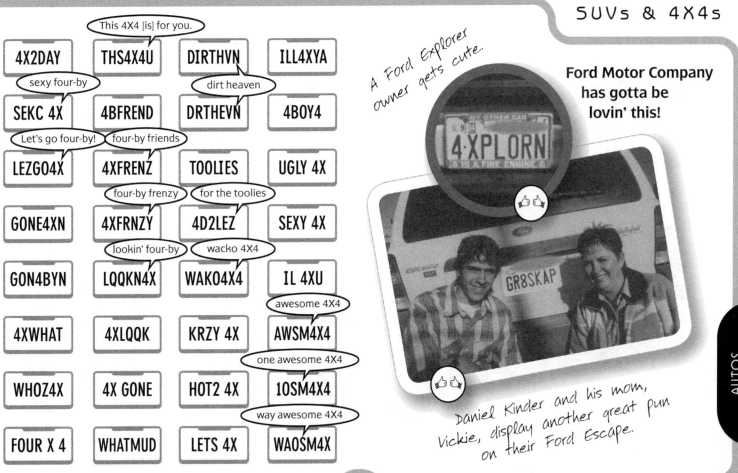

Ford Motor Company has gotta be lovin' this!

4·XPLORN

GR8SKAP

Daniel Kinder and his mom, Vickie, display another great pun on their Ford Escape.

AUTOS

"Z" Only Way to Fly!

We don't have room to feature all the cool auto makes that are rolling on the road. But all of them deserve a clever plate. Let's finish with some plates from Nissan "Z cars." With a name like that, they just beg for creative plates.

Did you see the Z go by?

In case you missed it, that was a 350 Z passin' you.

AUTOS

The Personalized Plate Capital of the World

What do you want to bet this driver is from Vegas?

Where is the personalized plate capital of the world?

It has to be Las Vegas, Nevada. Not only do they have millions of visitors each year, but it has been reported to me that over 100,000 personalized plates have been issued in the Las Vegas metropolitan area. I have seen six personalized plates at one time at a Las Vegas intersection. Pull into any parking lot there and you are bound to see plate creativity galore.

The Nevada DMV said that there was an 80% increase in personalized plate applications after my first book, *California Traffic Talk*, appeared in stores in the Las Vegas area in 1989.

Random plates seen in Vegas:

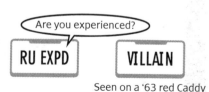

Are you experienced?

RU EXPD

VILLAIN

Seen on a '63 red Caddy

"I'll Bet That's the Governor's Car!"

We were driving down I-15 when I spotted a black Lincoln with smoked windows. I thought, "Wouldn't it be great to get a photo of the governor of the state of Utah in the book?" So I followed it for several miles. As the car pulled in to valet parking at a Hilton hotel, sure enough, out stepped ... Dan Thomas—not the governor! (Dan says his plate fakes out the best of them.)

Dan Thomas poses with Kath Giles by his attention-getting plate.

Two of My All-time Favorite License Plates

If I had to pick two of the most fascinating license plates I've ever encountered, they would be:

H2OUUP2   and   **IRIGHTI**

(This one was submitted by financial planner
Dave Cottrell, email: dcottrell3805w@wfgmail.com.)

Now, can you get these? It took me weeks and I suffered severe lack of sleep and brain cramp over these two.

(Answers below)

ANSWERS: **H2OUUP2** = "Water you up to?" **IRIGHTI** = "right between the eyes"

61

Sports Fans Take to the Streets

Real sports fans don't miss any opportunity to show their devotion to their team or their sport. On the following pages are examples of fans who wear their loyalty in plain view. See if you can top these!

Root for us!

ROOT 4S

A Raiders fan says it loud and proud.

Local Rivalries

This Caddy driver is obviously a fan of Brigham Young University (BYU), archrivals of the University of Utah (U of U).

At first, you would think Jeff Brown's plate says "Why hate her?" — as in ex-wife, etc. But closer inspection reveals that he is a die-hard University of Utah fan — archrivals of BYU, known locally as "the Y." (Great plate, Jeff!)

SPORTS

Great "Passing" Plays

In the stadium, on the couch, or on the road, football fans display their passion.

There's no mistaking what game or team this driver likes!

FOOTBAL

NFL FAN

PUNT

GO LONG

ENDZONE

TUCHDWN

FLDGOAL

1STNTEN

1ST N10

HLFTIME

GO49ERS

LOV49RS

GO 9RZ

GO49RZ

9RZ FAN

GO4T9RZ

TTTT9RZ

9RZRULE

Our license plate search
tells us the most dedicated fans out there
are the 49ers fans. They're definitely
licensed to kick some booty!

SPORTS

FOOTBALL

PACKERS   DOLFINS   GO RAMS   COWBOYZ

CHRGERZ

RAIDERZ

Just think — tomorrow there will be 27,000 football fans applying for this same plate in 49 states.

Okay, so he didn't win any spelling bees as a kid, but he's smart enough to root for the Raiders!

In case the one on the left is already taken in your state, here are some alternative spellings:

CHARJRS   CHARJRZ   CHARGRS   CHARGRZ   CHRGRS   CHRJRS   CHRGERS

SPORTS

This Chicago Bears fan leaves no doubt where his loyalty lies, sugar.

Love those Bears.
(But what about them Cubs?)

SPORTS

The All-American Sport

What's more American than baseball? Why, plate reading, of course!

Ah, there we have the Cubs!

This University of Utah women's baseball coach takes his work with him every night when he drives home.

SPORTS

STERIKE

STEERYK

YER OUT

YER OUT

HEZSAFE

FASTBAL

3 N 1

ARBY I — RBI

FASBALL

CURVBAL

CRVBALL

STRIKE3

SPITBAL

HOMERUN

HO MRUN

RBI MVP

SLUGGER

MUDVL 9 — Mudville Nine

SPORTS

Hoopin' It Up

If basketball is your game, you can stand tall with a slam-dunk plate like these.

Tonia Oxborrow, super school teacher and girls' basketball ref "scores" with the perfect plate!

NBA ROX	AIR BALL	DBLDRBL	NBA FAN
SUMBBAL	SWISH4U	HOOPS	NBALUVR
DUNK IT	HOOOOPS	NBAISOK	4DBULLS
TIP OFF			SUNSROK
ALL NET			LKRSFAN

Foursome for "Fore!"

Golfers love to putt around with their custom plates proudly on display, but when it comes to thinking up clever plate ideas, they're no duffers!

BADGLFR

DUH FER

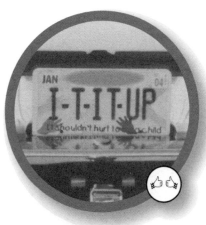

BADGOL4

BUMGOL4

We've all heard of a "black widow," but now we introduce the "golf widow." What a tangled web she weaves through traffic!

But Tiger would go at least 36!

you know, if someone made a car called a Titleist, they'd make a fortune off of these golfers!

Let's hope we're talking about a golf game and not heads — or tires!

SPORTS

Tennis Players Cause Traffic Jams

Tennis players seem to have a knack for some of the most clever, complicated plates.

Anyone for tennis?

Gaye Williamson sports one of the best tennis plates ever seen in North America.

Tennis for me.

Who says you can't cram three words and four syllables into seven characters?

Tennis, anyone?

tennis player

10SPLYR

Know why they call it "40 love" in tennis? Neither do we!

Of course, you don't have to limit yourself to just one sport. This driver crams two onto a single plate.

SPORTS

The Greatest Snow on Earth

Ski addicts know there's only one reason to have a car, and that's to get up to the ski resort! So of course you'll see their passion displayed on their license plates.

Please let him pass, dear. He's a ski pro.

Now we've seen everything.
First there was Al-Anon, then
Narc-Anon, now Ski-Anon?

If you're a beach bum this probably wouldn't be a good idea . . .

We've heard of DPOOPOO and deep other stuff, but now we've heard everything! Damond Holsinger and his son Lander show off their fun plate.

SPORTS

No Business Like Snow Business

One day I was sitting at the parking lot of the small Provo, Utah, airport (no, there's not a larger one either) and noticed a new white Jeep Cherokee that pulled onto the tarmac. Its plates read **SNOWBIZ**, and I thought what a great addition to this book! About a minute later a beautiful private jet (a rare Piaggio Avanti) pulled up and parked by the Jeep (just like in the movies!). As several people got out of the sleek jet, I noticed the lady in the Jeep give this big fellow a hug. They seemed to be in a good mood, so I just kind of wandered over and introduced myself. I found out that the group had just returned from a hunting trip to Canada and the lady in the Jeep was picking up her husband and some friends. I told them about this upcoming book and they were more than gracious to pose for these shots. I found out they were originally from Danville, California, and have a home in prestigious Deer Valley Resort near Park City, Utah (yes, this

is where the 2002 Olympics took place). Dr. Dar Datwyler, a retired orthodontist, and his wife Ellie think there is literally no business like SNOWBIZ! (It's amazing what first impressions personalized plates can leave—heck, I thought they owned every ski resort in Utah!)

Dr. Dar Datwyler
and his wife Ellie

Profile of a Personalized Plate Owner

These are common traits that all personalized license plate owners possess:

1. They are not afraid to be noticed.

2. Most admit that they spent days, weeks, or months, coming up with **the** perfect plate combination.

3. Many experience frustration and anxiety wondering if they chose the right plate combination.

4. Within a very short amount of time they realize that conversations arise regarding their plates constantly—at the gas station, grocery store, stadium parking lot—wherever they go.

5. They are friendly, personable, and possess a high degree of humor!

6. They also understand that since their car stands out in traffic, it only makes sense to be a more courteous driver.

7. They also tend to be more successful in their respective businesses and careers.

8. Whether they realize it or not, they have the "Law of Attraction" working in their favor. (This law is predicated on the theory that they will meet more people to do business with and with whom they share similar interests—"like attracts like"—therefore contributing to fattening their wallets.)

9. They are more likely to keep their cars clean and in good condition.

10. Since they are at the car wash more frequently, they meet other people circulating the wealth!

Fish Tales

Every fisherman has a tale. Many like to put them on their license plates.

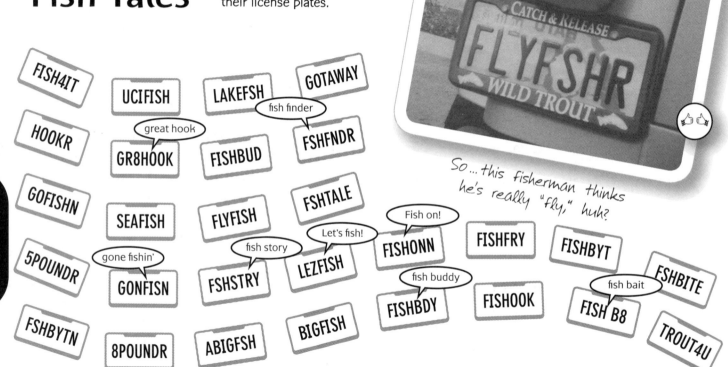

FISH4IT

UCIFISH

LAKEFSH

GOTAWAY

fish finder
FSHFNDR

HOOKR

great hook
GR8HOOK

FISHBUD

GOFISHN

SEAFISH

FLYFISH

FSHTALE

CATCH & RELEASE
FLYFSHR
WILD TROUT

So... this fisherman thinks he's really "fly," huh?

Fish on!
FISHONN

FISHFRY

FISHBYT

5POUNDR

gone fishin'
GONFISN

fish story
FSHSTRY

Let's fish!
LEZFISH

fish bait
FISH B8

FSHBITE

fish buddy
FISHBDY

FISHOOK

FSHBYTN

8POUNDR

ABIGFSH

BIGFISH

TROUT4U

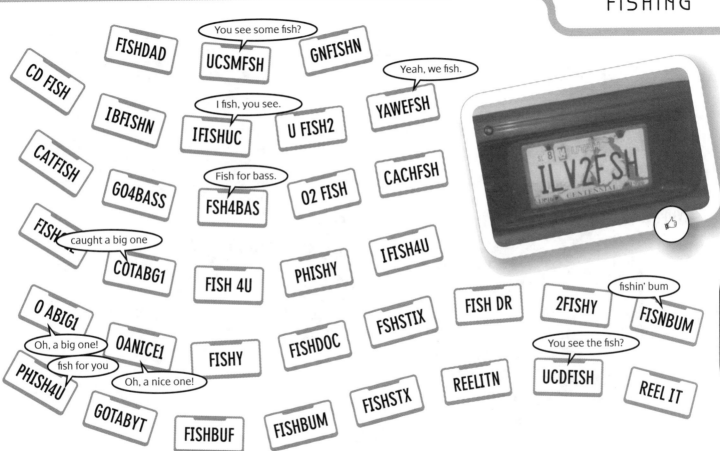

High Flyers

Whether flying high or flying low, pilots love to fly, and it shows—on their plates

born to fly
BRN2FLY

28000FT

FLYUPHI

FLYBOY
MOUNTAINEER

I fly, do you?
IFLYDOU

I'm a pilot.
IMAPILT

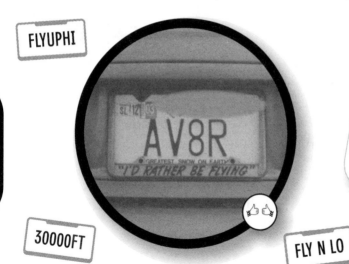

30000FT

FLY N LO

This driver loves to fly — and it shows!

Terry Spinks reveals his true passion on his Cadillac SUV.

Terry's "other car" is a Cessna Conquest.

SPORTS

Recreational Plate Use

Whatever your favorite sport or recreational activity may be, tell the world with a creative personalized license plate. You'll find inspiring examples on the following pages.

I do! I do! I do!

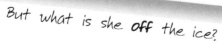

But what is she **off** the ice?

SPORTS

You know how many thumbs-up they get from other scuba fanatics?

We didn't see any wild hogs running around; however, we did see a couple of Harleys wallowing in the mud off in the distance.

Meet Lori Hansen (middle) and her daughters, Karly (left) and Sarah (right). These chicks really make waves!

DUKTWUK

You mean there's a possibility that you could do it for me?

Maybe up to the 7 Eleven and back — but **forever**?

SPORTS

Some people are into fitness; others are just into throwing fits.

SPORTS

And we're here to …

Is this the opposite of Miller time?

SPORTS

Winners and Losers

Like you'd put "LOSER" on a license plate. (Uh-oh, we might have just given somebody another idea!)

Now, here's a real winner:

SPORTS

How I Lost $50 in a Las Vegas Restaurant

I grew up in Las Vegas, Nevada. Back in 1988, my brother Dave and I were sitting in the Palace Station Restaurant discussing the cover design of my first book, *California Traffic Talk*. We were thinking of the perfect plate to go on the front cover when a man at the next table, who must have overheard our conversation, said, "So, what are you—some kind of license plate expert?"

I said, "Well, you know we are putting this book out with 50,000 of America's best license plates." And I said proudly that we had researched over 3 million plates to get the best of the best. So I said, "Yeah, we have deciphered some pretty challenging license plates."

With that he said, "Well, I've got one you can't figure out, and I'll even bet you $50 you can't figure it out."

Now here it goes (me and my big mouth). I put $50 on the table and so did he. Then he wrote down a plate combination that read NEDKCME .

I looked at this approximately 10 seconds and realized I was in trouble. I said, "Give me a few more minutes and I'll have the answer for you." About 15 minutes later I had to confess to him that he had me and my 50 bucks.

After I said uncle a couple of times (not really), he took my $50 bill and then he told me the answer. He said that it belonged to his dentist in California and that it read "Any decay, see me"! I am just happy to say that through the years I have become a much more effective plate reader and haven't lost any bets since.

License Plates as Marketing Tools

Creative plates are a great way to attract new business. After all, the plate is actually a small "billboard" that sets you apart from your competition. There are countless times in traffic, in the supermarket parking lot, or at the gas station where people will comment about your plate and find out that you have the product or services they're looking for. Just ask any business owner who has a creative plate, and you'll see what we mean!

How many potential customers or clients are literally passing you by because you don't have the right conversation starter? Put a creative plate on your car, and watch the magic unfold!

Financial planner, David Cottrell, greets everyone he passes with his friendly plate.

BUSINESS

For a Ferrari or a Porsche, yes.
But for a Honda Civic?
I don't think so!

The Royal Road to Riches

Royal and Meda West keep their eight martial arts studios kickin' by using all the tools of "guerilla" marketing—including vehicle graphics and, of course, a custom license plate fit for a king.

Believe it or not, both of these plates were shot
on opposite sides of the same parking lot!
Who **says** cars can't talk?

A favorite for multi-level marketers.

. . . and she still
said no!

Whatever Floats Your Boat

Clark Heringer, owner of Heringer Marine in Orem, Utah, uses creative plates to keep his dealership sailing smooth.

This trailer holds all the four wheelers and other toys.

Love Powell!

This one, on his Chevy Suburban, refers to Lake Powell, a popular boating destination.

Clark and his wife like to sneak out in their Corvette "getaway" car.

Drue and Carolyn Burkhalter, owners of the Kid Zone store in Las Vegas, have turned their Acura into a driving billboard — for around $60.

A great example of how to integrate a personalized plate into an overall marketing program.

Green Is Sprouting Up Everywhere!

I often get asked what's the best plate I've ever seen. That's a tough question — I've seen so many great ones. But one of the most "valuable" plate combos is the one on Jim and Marie Dahlen's H2 Hummer. I spotted the plate on the freeway and called the toll-free number. Two weeks later my video crew was at their beautiful home to uncover the incredible story behind their BGREEN1 plate. Go to our web site (**www.licenseplatefun.com**) and click on their link, or go directly to their web site (**www.bgreen1.com**) for the whole story. You'll be amazed when you meet who drives this Hummer!

Jim and Marie Dahlin are turning the curative powers of healthy greens into green and spreading the good word every time they took down the highway.

BUSINESS

For exciting contest info and prizes 100 visit www.licenseplatefun.com.

The Game of Work

Chuck Coonradt should know a thing or two about making work fun. After all, his best-selling book, *The Game of Work*, tells readers how they can enjoy work as much as play. Chuck regularly speaks to Fortune 500 companies about the principles in his book. And he practices what he preaches, as you can see from his fun plate that reminds everyone on the road that he wrote the book on making work fun!

Look for a mint-green Porsche passing you at 100 miles per hour with this plate. You'll know it's Chuck.

What Personalized Plate Owners Know —That You Don't

When was the last time you saw a personalized license plate? Yesterday? This morning? Maybe there's one in front of you right now. With almost 11 million of these "mini billboards," and legal in all 50 states—yeah, it's kind a of hard not to notice them. Believe it or not, we are actually "conditioned" to look for them.

The next time you're watching a movie and the car pulls onto the scene, notice how you instinctively zoom in on the license plate—you know, that quick glance to see if it possibly has a personalized plate? We do the same thing in traffic—especially when certain kinds of cars come into view. Perhaps we ought to give this quick glance a name. How about "Plate Quickie"? Ok, we'll get back to that later.

In America and many other countries of the world, people are actually **addicted** to reading the ever-famous, personalized license plate. After researching over 4 million such plates and interviewing thousands of people that own them, my conclusion is that they are actually "personalized logos," and we all know that the logo is king (queen).

The dentist whose car has 2TH DOC meets more new patients on accident (no pun intended) than other dentists do on purpose.

A divorce attorney who has **ILSUYRX** ("I'll sue your ex") will be introduced to more bad marriages while getting a tank of gas than his yellow page ad may attract in a month.

Looking for a date? **UB SINGL** on your plate would be stiff competition for any on-line dating website.

So what do these plate owners know that you don't? They simply know how to get your attention, keep you in suspense, state their case and put a smile on your face—all within 5 seconds. Personalized plate? Logo? Maybe the original "text message"? Nah, it's just a "Plate Quickie"!

If you want to meet people for business or pleasure, a personalized license plate is one of the least expensive and most effective ways to advertise. Ad agencies spend millions of dollars trying to get your attention, but it can't even come close to what a personalized plate can do for you during morning drive time.

Want a perfect example of how license plates help connect people? Check out the plates below and find out how I met the amazing entrepreneur who owns them. (See pages 136 and 137.)

Plate owner Barbara Williams has written over 50 books for children, including the best-seller *Titanic Crossing*, which sold over 1,000,000 copies. Her new book, *Albert's Impossible Toothache*, should be a smash hit, too! RYTE-ON, Barbara!

The Bigger the Boys, the Bigger the Toys

Glade McDonald is one of America's number one Snap-on tool dealers. He calls his truck the "toy store."

Personalized Plates Hit Pay Dirt

Jewelry store owner Richard Wilson mixes work and play with his fleet of Minis sporting vanity plates, Richard has been a plate aficionado for decades. When he buys a new car, he doesn't consider the purchase complete until he has also equipped it with its own unique creative plate. For his jewelry store business he gives several of his college-age employees a company car—a Mini plastered with promotional graphics and, of course, a witty plate—for them to drive all around town, giving Wilson Diamonds exposure everywhere they go. Are you asking yourself, "Now, why didn't I think of that?"

Two Hot Items

Melana Child shows off a plate advertising Cafe Rio—a Mexican grill renowned throughout the Southwest for tasty, spicy dishes.

The Professional Edge

When hiring a professional, people go with who they know. Traditional mass-market advertising and marketing don't work as well for people who offer specialized professional services. As a professional, most of your business comes by word-of-mouth referrals. You know how critically important it is to build a wide network of acquaintances.

A creative license plate is a great way to introduce yourself to thousands of people who would otherwise never hear of you. It sets you apart as being accomplished, "with it," and approachable.

The following pages show examples of professionals at their best.

Chris Dexter, principal of
Dexter & Dexter, Attorneys at Law,
advertises the firm everywhere he drives.
He says the plate brings them
a lot of business.

Attorneys Say the Funniest Things!

They're clever, they're brash, and they're loaded with cash. So if you find yourself staring at one of these plates on the back of a late-model luxury car, you're probably eating a lawyer's dust!

See my attorney.
CMYATTY

I'll sue your ex!
ILSUYRX

WLDATTY

Get an attorney.
GTNATTY

IL SU4 U

GOTATTY

LAW MAN

ILSU 4U

GTALWYR

TAXATTY

THEATTY

WHOSUDU

trial attorney
TRYLATY

Injured? See me!
NJRDCME

See you in court!
CUNCORT

per[sonal] injury
PERNJRY

attorney [at] large
ATTYLRG

Why not sue too?
YNOTSU2

back in court
BKNCORT

GOTSUED

See a lawyer.
CALAWYR

1ATTY4U

TAX ESQ

YNOTSU2

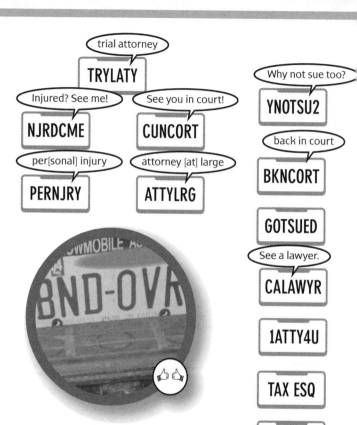

This **has** to be an attorney's plate!

ATORNEE ATERNEE ATTERNY ATORNIE ATOURNY

INCOURT

Here are five ways to spell attorney. Can you think of others?

N COURT

But, your Honor . . .

THE LAW BTYRONR

Your Honor . . .
YRHONOR

Your Honor . . .
YRAHNER

Your Honor . . .
YR ONNR

If at first you don't succeed at getting your plate
approved, you can always appeal to another spelling.

YRATRNY YORATTY IOBJECT YORATTY

LOY YER LAW YER HABIUS WE SU 4U

COURTD8 CORT D8 BNDOVER LAWYR4U

ATTYGUY ATNYGUY SSTAIND ITSTHLW

ATTY 4U ATNYGAL MYATRNY

IDENYIT
BARTON J. WARREN

There's no denying we're on an
attorney's tail here!

attorney lady
ATNYL80 ATTYLDY CANSU4U

tough attorney
TUFATTY

OCCUPATIONS

Everyone Knows Accountants Are Bor…Exciting!

OCCUPATIONS

CPATWRK

TAX BRK

T heir work may be boring, but these guys come up with some mighty clever plates!

UNEDCPA

You need [a] CPA.

UNIQCPA

TAX CPA

ID DUCT	WILDCPA	CPAQT4U	NEEDCPA	CP AZE
DDUKSHN (deduction)	ACCTANT (CPA ahead)	CPA QT	CPAWORK	COOLCPA
DDUCSHN	CPAAHED	RITEOFF	CPALADY (CPA lady)	CPA STUD

MY CPA

TAXTIPS

ACE CPA	I ADD4U (CPA, cutie pie)	RYT OFF	CPA L80	CPAAAAA	YOURCPA	CEPEAA	CPA MOM
TAX CPA	CPAQTPI	WRITOFF	SMRTCPA	CP YEA	YOR CPA	IMYRCPA (I'm your CPA.)	CPAATTY

CPA ACE   THE CPA   YER CPA   I ADM UP

I add 'em up.

TAX4BUX   CPABOSS

1HOTCPA   CPA BIZ   CPA GUY   CPA KID

HOT CPA   GOTCPA   CPA GAL   OK CPA

AHOTCPA   ADDS UP   IMA CPA   SUPR CPA

1TAXPRO   ITADSUP   IMACPA2   DDUCT4U

ITOKCPA   CME4CPA   CPA DAD   ATAXPRO

I talk CPA.

CPATALK   CPAFOX   CPA FOX   KOOLCPA

no more tax

NEEDCPA   NOMOTAX   LESS TAX   KQQLCPA

Patrick McCarthy's BMW instantly tells us three things about him: He's a CPA, he's successful, and he's creative. Way to go!

TAXTIME

TAXCASH

OCCUPATIONS

OCCUPATIONS

Incurably Funny Doctors

With so many patients, you'd think doctors wouldn't have the patience to come up with witty plates. But these will keep you in stitches.

Now, there's one smooooth operator!

DR IS IN	DR IS N	GAS DOC
ORTHODR	BONE DR	BONEDOC
MD 4YOU	CLNC MD	EMER DR
MD4 YOU	CMND AM	FAMLYDR
THE DOC	BRAINDR	FAMLYMD
BABY MD	SURGEON	ER MD
LADY MD	PAINDOC	I OPR 8
OBGYN DR	NEURODR	POOR MD

See me in the morning.

I DOC

MAD MD

See an eye doctor.
CNI DOC

SKIN DR

ZIT DOC

IDOC 4U

See a doctor.
CADOCTR

FMLYDOC

FUN DOC

For obstetricians:

DUE D8

DO DATE

DO D8

OCCUPATIONS

1FUNDOC

MDFOR U

IMA DR

IMN MD

I am an MD.

I am a baby doctor.

IMABBDR

See an eye doctor.

CNEYEDR

See an eye doctor.

CNI DR

HEADDOC

ORTHOMD

EYE DOC

NMD 4U

You see an MD to be.

UCNMD2B

N MD 2B

Chiropractors Straighten Us Out

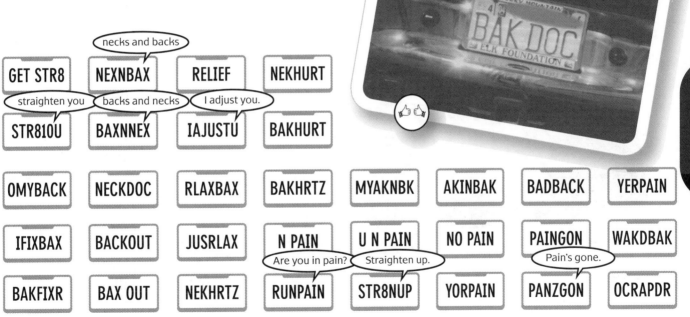

necks and backs

GET STR8	NEXNBAX	RELIEF	NEKHURT

straighten you · backs and necks · I adjust you.

STR810U	BAXNNEX	IAJUSTU	BAKHURT

OMYBACK	NECKDOC	RLAXBAX	BAKHRTZ	MYAKNBK	AKINBAK	BADBACK	YERPAIN
IFIXBAX	BACKOUT	JUSRLAX	N PAIN	U N PAIN	NO PAIN	PAINGON	WAKDBAK

Are you in pain? · Straighten up. · Pain's gone.

BAKFIXR	BAX OUT	NEKHRTZ	RUNPAIN	STR8NUP	YORPAIN	PANZGON	OCRAPDR

OCCUPATIONS

OCCUPATIONS

Sink Your Teeth into These!

See me before decay.

CME B4DK

👍👍

A plate similar to this one cost the author $50 in a wager. See page 92.

Attention dentists, orthodontists, and dental technicians: Looking for a plate idea that doesn't bite? Try these!

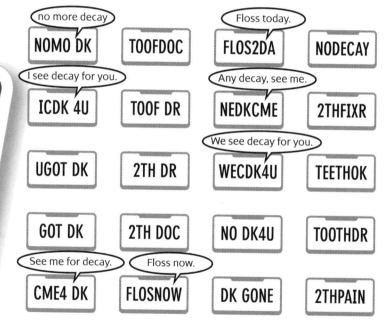

no more decay
NOMO DK

TOOFDOC

Floss today.
FLOS2DA

NODECAY

I see decay for you.
ICDK 4U

TOOF DR

Any decay, see me.
NEDKCME

2THFIXR

UGOT DK

2TH DR

We see decay for you.
WECDK4U

TEETHOK

GOT DK

2TH DOC

NO DK4U

TOOTHDR

See me for decay.
CME4 DK

Floss now.
FLOSNOW

DK GONE

2THPAIN

2THMEDC

2TH·FERY — tooth fairy

2THACHE

2TH AKE

PRLY·YTS

Flash those pearly whites!

GUM DR

2THHURT

2THOUCH

2TH HZ

DRSMILE

1DENTST

OMYTOOF

2THURTZ

IH8 DK

FLOSS M

ORTHODR

SMYLDOC

IH8DCAY

FLOSS M

OMY 2TH

SMILDOC

YR2THDR

DK NOMO — decay no more

The author caught Aubree Park with Chris Erekson out cruisin' in Chris's dad's four-by-four. Dr. David Erekson tells everyone to "open wide!"

OCCUPATIONS

OCCUPATIONS

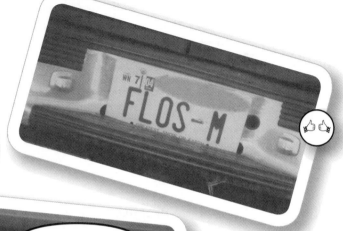

PERIODR

wire bender

WIRBNDR

I fix smiles.

GUM DOC

SMILEDR

How about fixin' the one on my ex-wife's face?

ADENTST

License and Registration, Please!

You think **you're** nervous when a police officer pulls you over? That's nothing compared to what **he's** feeling as he approaches your door. He's sweating like an Arkansas politician. He doesn't know whether he's going to face a homicidal maniac or a just a bad case of PMS on Prozac. All he knows is what he can get from running your license plate. If your plate is fun and creative, though, he doesn't even need to run it to know that you're likely to be a harmless, fun-loving driver. It will help put him at ease. Who knows, it might even put him in a cheery enough mood that he'll let you off easy. Let's just call it traffic ticket insurance. It's worth a shot, don't you think?

Better be glad cops can't write tickets for boring plates. A **Corolla** driver might be able to get off easy, but a **Carrera** driver? They'd throw the book at you!

OCCUPATIONS

Real Estate Prose

When placing your advertising, don't forget the three "L"s: location, location, and location. While your competition may be spending big bucks on bus billboard advertising, you can get a similar impact for next to nothing with your own little "ad" on the back of your mobile office.

	homes (spelled backward)			
NO RENT	Z3MOH	GOT HOUS	HOMEBOY	DEALMKR
ISELAND (I sell land.)	HOMFIND	BNAHOME	DNTRENT (Don't rent.)	IT SOLD
LANDEAL	NDAHOME	ILSELU1	YRENT	SELFAST
ICDEALS	HOME4U2	HOMSELR	YNOTBUY	SOLDFST

OCCUPATIONS

With a tag like this, you're bound to become a household name in your market!

GOTHOME   AHOME4U   HAVHOME   YNOTBY1   REALST8 *(real estate)*   OWNHOME   RENTSUX   1A HOME *(Wanna home?)*

TV Personalities

If you happen to be a news anchor, you can't help having people gawk at you in public. So why not flaunt it with a clever plate on your car?

NEWZAT6	ON AT 5

BACK2U	NWSTORY

NEWSACE

NEWSTRY	NWZTORY	ONDNEWS	CTHNEWS

FILMAT5	NEWSGAL	THENEWS	WATCHIT

Did you see the news?

THE FAX	NEWSGUY	NEW ZZ	JUCDNUZ

Dave Courvosier, a popular former news anchor in Las Vegas, has the plate CUONTV. I've always thought that was a great one for a TV personality.

Can You CD DJ?

L et's not forget the folks who keep us entertained in the car—the drive-time deejays and talk-show hosts. Here are some ideas for the "ideas" people.

STAY2ND	MGA HRTZ	KQQL DJ	DJNDAIR	AMDRIVE	ON AIR
RADIODJ	TUNE N	TRNMEON	TUNE2FM	DRIVTYM	AM DJ
RAYDODJ	FMDRIVE	UCD DJ	ONAIRDJ	LISN UP	FM DJ

Movie Matches and TV Trivia

Personalized plates are everywhere. Let's see how many personalized plates you have noticed prominently displayed on TV and film.

1 Can you name a television series that used a close-up of a personalized plate to identify the name of the show in the opening credits? (Hint: It was about a Los Angeles law firm.)

2 Can you name the television series with a handsome private detective in a classic, red Ford Thunderbird and a personalized plate? What did the plate say?

3 In the motion picture *Arthur*, with Dudley Moore, what did the personalized plate say on his Rolls Royce?

4 In what Sylvester Stallone motion picture was `50 MERC` seen?

5 In National Lampoon's Mafia spoof *The Don's Analyst*, with Kevin Pollak, Angie Dickinson and Robert Loggia, a black Jaguar prominently displayed what personalized license plate?

6 In the movie *Con Air*, with Nicolas Cage, one of the detectives drove a classic, silver Corvette convertible. What did the license plate say?

7 What was on the proctologist's plate that Kramer mistakenly received in the mail in the famous *Seinfeld* episode? Honk your horn if you know the answer!

ANSWERS: 1. LA Law 2. Vegas, TANNA (Robert Urich played Dan Tanna) 3. ARTHUR 4. Nighthawks 5. BRKALEG 6. AZZKIKR

CON.COM	MAC GUY	PUTRPRO
WWW	PROPHED	HTMLPRO
HACKER	MEGAWHT	XML PRO
PUTRGUY	GIGABYT	GIGAWIZ
BYTEWHT	MEGAWIZ	BYTEWIZ
MAC GAL	PC H8R	SQL PRO

It's All Geek to Me

With the dot-com bubble bursting, computer geeks can use all the help they can get finding work. Here are some license plate ideas for turning your beater into a rolling billboard. We've also thrown in some e-mail related plates just for fun.

Here's someone who can hack it.

Chicks in the Mail

When you're a letter carrier, you're used to being noticed and welcomed wherever you go. So it's no wonder that postal workers Sandra and Michelle strut their stuff on the road as well. Gives a whole new meaning to "going postal" ...

SEKCONE

SEKCTRY   SEXYCEC

Secretaries Speak Their Minds

Ding! Who's next?

Talk about an icy reception . . .

One of the best secretary's plates I've ever seen was in Las Vegas. It read: XEC SEC

Pat Pritchett, personal assistant to WordPerfect founder Alan Ashton, is on the road so much that she calls her minivan "Pat's office."

OCCUPATIONS

Occupational Therapy

No matter what your occupation, a creative license plate is a great way to let the public know what you do. Personalized plates are wonderful conversation starters, and conversations lead to more business. Check out the occupation-related plates on the following pages for inspiration.

. . . but I don't do windows.

Every custom plate tells a story. We're guessing the driver of this car tells quite a few.

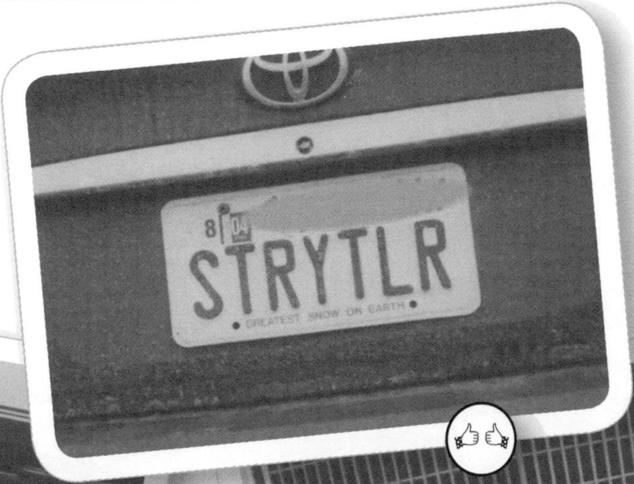
STRYTLR
GREATEST SNOW ON EARTH

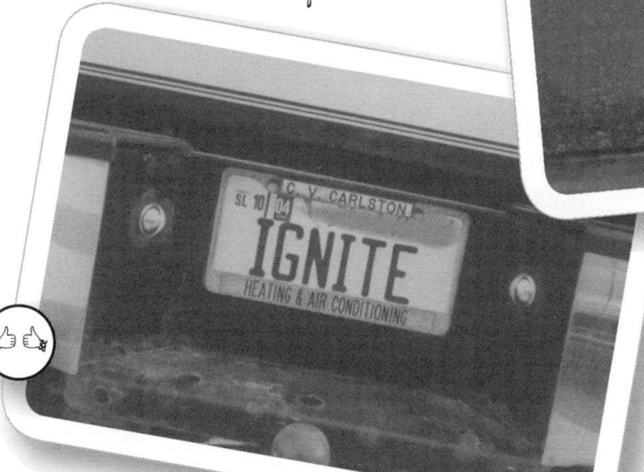
C.V. CARLSTON
IGNITE
HEATING & AIR CONDITIONING

How many furnace guys can get their potential customers fired up like this? Exactly one in each state.

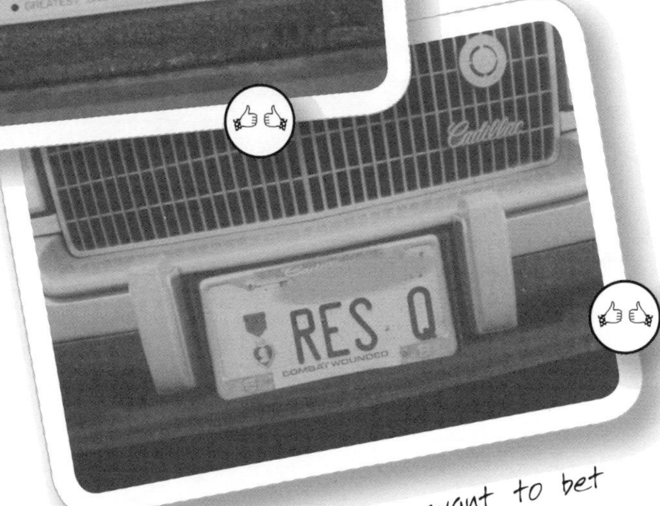
RES Q
COMBAT WOUNDED

Lost? What do you want to bet this motorist can help?

There's no midwife crisis here.

With a plate like this, this plumber can rest assured his business won't go down the drain.

Bruce Geurts is "licensed" to do business! Good job!

An astronomer?
Hollywood analyst?
Boxer?

FLASH THE CASH!

Tyler Christiansen, Vice President of corporate banking for Zions Bank, gets a lot of "interest" with his plate.

Flash a Trucker

If you woke up this morning, had breakfast, got in your car, drove to the gym, stopped off at Starbucks for a quickie, went to the office, worked on your computer, talked on your cell phone, or any of a number of the thousand things we all do each day—thank a trucker. That's right, these are the men and women sittin' up in those big rigs, driving down the freeway, hauling all kinds of stuff to make life easier for all of us.

Truckers see everything. Some of the best plates in this book were spotted by truckers.

The next time you pass a trucker, flash this book at 'em to let 'em know that you appreciate them keeping the economy rolling. If they honk back, chances are they've got a copy of this book, too!

This tribute brought to you by Andrus Transportation Services, 1-800-888-5838.

Telltale Signs of Greatness

Mitch with his Bentley

Mitch Huhem is one of those amazing, eminently successful people, like his friend Donald Trump, that most of us only hear about but never actually meet. Thanks to Ned Chidester and Don Davis, I was introduced to Mitch because of his personalized plates. For Mitch, like so many successful entrepreneurs, creativity, drive, flashy cars, personalized plates, and success—they all go together. He owns a fleet of exotic cars, all emblazoned with creative plates.

Mitch Huhem is one of the world's visionary people. His high-energy "team player" approach to everything he does empowers those around him to achieve their dreams and goals. During our photo shoot, he taught me his mantra: "I can do it, yes I can; you can do it, yes you can; we can do it, yes we can." As a motivational speaker,

Mitch and his daughter Elisa with his Mercedes Sk AMG

Mitch is breathtaking (and incredibly funny, too). As a business idea person, he is someone to emulate. If you are interested in growing your business and increasing your income, put this book down right now and let the Internet introduce you to Mitch. Just do a Yahoo search on "Mitch Huhem in Utah" and see all the cool stuff that shows up. Click on the song he wrote, "Born to Be Great," performed by Jared Osmond and Jenny Frogley, and listen to the inspiring lyrics.

Mitch Huhem knows what so many highly successful people know: Personalized plates help put you on the fast track to success!

Don't Forget the Creative Plate!

Success and creative license plates both run in the Huhem family. (See previous two pages.) Mitch's brother Victor is a successful real estate and contract attorney. Like his brother, Victor is a firm believer that a nice vehicle is not completely dressed until it has that finishing touch—the right personalized license plate.

Traffic Greetings

Folks are a-greetin' each other all the time behind the wheel, whether it's with a wave, a single-finger salute, a forefinger to the forehead, or a forearm and fist. On the following pages are ideas for kindly greetings you could put on the back of your car.

		Hey, [what]'s up?	I'm okay. And you?	
HOW U	HEY U	HEY SUP	IM OKNU	HISEZME
HI BABY	JSAYNHI *(jus' sayin' hi)*	HI YALL	HIFOLKS	WHO U
HI YA	SAY N HI	HEYYALL	WHATSAY	HOWUDO

THEMES

Let's get things movin', say Carrie Bradshaw, her daughter Melissa, and friend Bobbie Jo. Melissa's car sports a plate that says HOMBY12, Carrie's husband's plate says CACHUP and her other daughter has one that says HI YA.

The Peep Show

Whether it's catching a secret glance or casting a withering glare, so much of the communication with your fellow motorists is through eye contact. Here are some ideas to let the looky-loos know you're on to them.

CUPEEPN	DNTPEEK	MMLQQKY	LOOKELU
CUPEEKN	UBPEEKN	UBLQQKN	TH LQQK
ICUPEKD	YUBLUKN	UBLOOKN	HELQQKD
PK BOO	OH LQQK	LQQKATU	LQQKAWA
JS1LOOK	YALQQKD	LUKNATU	YNTLQQK

But honey, can you **hear** me? That's the deal!

I. SEE U

CUPEEPN

Sabrina Cool (yes, that's really her last name) sees everyone peepin' as she tools on down the highway. Cool plate!

We're Outta Here!

Saying good-bye is so hard to do. On the next few pages are some classic parting shots.

BYE BYE	BYE NOW	YA BCNU	IL BCNU
CEEYALL	BYEYALL	BCNU OK	BYEUALL
BUNJOUR	C YOLL	BONJOUR	BYUWALL

Yeah, be seein' you.

'Bye, you all!

SEE YALL	CU L8 R	OKILCYA
SI YALL	GOTTAGO	OKIMGON
BYBY CU	BCNUL8R	BCNYALL
IL BCNU	ILBGOIN	W84 ME
C YALL	L8RDUDE	BYE4NOW
CUALLOK	L8RYALL	HEYL8R
C UALL	ILLBCNU	BCNU 2
CU ALL	BCNU OK	BUSY CU

Okay, I'm gone.

be seein' you later

Wait for me!

Later, y'all!

THEMES

I'm Late! I'm Late!

Always running late? Here are some plate ideas just in time for you. (See pages 254 and 255 for some more "late" plate ideas.)

IM LATE	IML8 RU

NEVER L8	IM L8	IMSOOL8	ONOIML8

L8 AGAIN	IM SO L8	DONTBL8	OL8AGIN

I'm later'n you!

I'm late! Are you too?

I'm late! I'm late!

IML8RNU	OHSO L8	IML8 RU2	WON'TBL8	IML8 ML8	OSO L8

THEMES

Pickup Lines (for Singles Only)

| CU AT 7 | CU 2NYT | MSAYBBY | FONE D8 |
| CU AT 6 | CU2NITE | JUSAYHI | LV2KOLU |

- See you tonight. → CU 2NYT
- Mmm ... Say, baby ... → MSAYBBY
- Jus' say hi. → JUSAYHI
- Love to call you! → LV2KOLU
- Did you say hi? → JUSAYHI

Hey, singles, what better way to catch the attention of the opposite sex than with a catchy plate? The next few pages feature a bunch of pickup lines. (No pickup required.)

Well, maybe.

4U1WOOD
UNITED NISSAN

1GR8GUY

That's what he says, but what about his ex-wife?

THEMES

You be single too?

Want a hubby?

Wanna date?

| UBSNGL2 | ILCUAT7 | WANAHBY | WANNAD8 | OYABABY | HIYABBY | KACHING | SINGAL | 1 A D8 |

Late for a date

Let's go out! You busy tonight?

| L84AD8 | SAHIBBY | MMMBABY | D8 NITE | OBBITSU | LZGOOUT | UBZ2NYT | OUTOND8 | CALL ME |

UMHI QT

AAHI QT

a date tonight

| AD82NYT | KOLMEOK | JSCOLME |

See you in a while.   Baby, don't be late.

| CUNA YL | BBDNBL8 | CU AT 7 |

Are you Cinderella?

Successful **SWM** seeks lady, 45 to 50, non-smoker, nondrinker. Kids okay (no gang members). Sense of humor required. Must like fishing or at least tolerate weekend absences. Must own boat and motor. Please send recent photo (of boat and motor). Call Frank at 801-671-9656.

SNGLSUX | CME4AD8 | 1HOT D8 | IMNHEAT | CELL M8 | CM4FUN | PHONEME | FONE ME | NETYMQT

SNGLLYF

CALL8R | HES D1 | OBMYQT | U2NITE

SNGLONE

SAYQTPI | RUD14ME | UNME BB | CU2 NYT

SNGL 1

EMELME | AZMEOUT

YBSNGL

CALL ME

HOTDATE

HI QTPI

ANMAL4U

you gotta like a guy who ain't afraid to come clean!

SNGLDAD

HEYQTPI

CHALKUP

SMOOCHR | OK HI QT | L8R QT | FUNCHIC

RUSINGL

SNGLGAL | SHES D1 | L8R OKQT | FUNDUDE

Quick: what word comes to mind? Survey says ... experience!

UBSNGL2

| YA LETS | ONADATE | 1 2 D8 | OUT4FUN | SURILGO | DATENYT | UAVLABL | OUT2NYT | MID 14U |

| ME NU QT | | D8 NITE | GOT N L8 | ON A D8 | UBZ2NYT | U UP4IT | L8DATE |

Why not call?

| D8 ME | YNTCALL | COLMEOK | LOOK CT | 1FUNGUY |

| ONA D8 | COMOVER |

| LOVE2D8 |

| GETA D8 |

| SAVE SEX |

| 1FUNGAL | DNT BL8 | TEASEME | LSGOOUT | CMONOVR | JUSCALL |

date on Friday

a date for you   See me for a date.

| 2SATSFY | REDYAT7 | JS1CALL | D8ONFRI | SINGL2 | CA MOVIE | AD8 4U | CME4AD8 | ASMEOUT |

THEMES

Please Leave a Message

In today's fast-paced society, we're always leaving messages — on voice mail, answering machines, and e-mail. So why not leave a message like this on your license plate as well? Just wait for the sound of the beep . . .

| LEAVMSG | LVAMESG | LEVAMSG |

ILMELYA	EMAILME	ILLEMEL	CHTLINE	SNDMAIL
GETMAIL	JUSEMEL	EMELADD	LEZCHAT	ILMELYA
IGOTMEL	EMAILYA	INSTMES	LESCHAT	CHKEMEL
CHKEMEL	CTHMAIL	INSTMSG	IE MAIL	UGOTMEL
UGOTMEL	PSHSEND	CHATLYN	SENDMEL	EMEL AD

Romance
on the Road

You see a lot of romance out on the road. Check out the romantic plates on the next few pages.

NLV4EVR

Well, cupcake, he'd better be, or you just wasted $55!

Glenwood Springs, Colorado

UN 6 04

WHTAWMN

ELK Mountain Motors

Makes you want to pull up alongside and check her out, doesn't it!

THEMES

Divorce insurance?

THEMES

Married, with plates:

Kristin Delatorre really is
a six-foot-tall blond.

Her husband goes
"Cuban style."

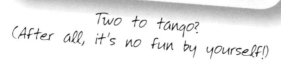

Two to tango?
(After all, it's no fun by yourself!)

Natalie's boyfriend said, "You either take that plate off your car, or this relationship is over." She said, "Gee, baby, I'm sure gonna miss you!"

THEMES

William and Betty Atkinson told me (in front of their dog, Angel) that they met back in 1974 in a bar in Lewiston, Idaho. Bill was from Idaho and Miss Betty was from Arkansas. (Now you know the rest of the story!)

"Wait For ME!"
Kent and Wieshia Ogaard wanted a fun plate to put on their bug.

A note from...

David Clough

We often get comments on our plate message. GREAT WAY TO MEET INTERESTING PEOPLE!

Dave & Betty Clough

O.K. to use our photo!

Dave Clough

My wife says she's the HUNY, but...

38-12-5

THEMES

Kiss and Tell

born to kiss

BRN2KIS

SAMOOCH

MWAH MWAH!
Tough one not to notice, huh?

No one likes a mooch,
but everyone likes a smooch!

THEMES

Entrepreneur extraordinaire Kandis Holley Howard poses by a very eye-catching plate on her Jeep. She has a unique business that produces and sells lip care products. Do they work? Find her at www.lips2kiss.com

This motorist always gets a couple of licks in!

THEMES

All You Need Is Love

Start paying attention to personalized plates and you'll quickly see there are a lot of love-themed plates.

No matter how you say it — or spell it — it always sounds nice!

Wait 'til I show Fred and Ethyl!

Of course, not all love is romantic . . .

Stay tuned ...

(On the way to happy hour!)

Seven Habits of Highly Creative License Plate Owners

1 When two or more drivers are going for the same parking spot, the creative plate owner will always be gracious, kind, and considerate, and let the other person have it.

2 If you ever need help with a flat tire, just look for the personalized plate owner—they're knowledgeable and properly equipped to help you out in your dilemma!

3 Left your jumper cables at home? Creative plate owners are always ready to jump you—errr, **help** you.

4 Out of gas on a lonely road? That's right—look for the personalized plate owner, and if they don't have an extra gallon in their trunk, they'll probably siphon out some from their tank right there on the spot!

5 Locked your keys in the car? Yep, that's right— they're always prepared with the perfect hanger to do the job or they'll offer you their cell phone to call the locksmith.

6 New in town and need directions? Ask a creative plate owner. If they don't know, they'll fake it until they find someone who does.

7 Stuck on a busy freeway—can't escape? You know creative plate owners will probably smile and wave as they let you over!

Take It from the Top

Whether your car is topless or not, you can't top plates like these for turning heads!

A BMW Z4 exposes itself.

Notice the trouble I went through to get this shot. TOPLSBJ — I don't get it. We'll have to do a full investigation.

THEMES

Plates That Made It Under the Censor's Radar

Every state has censors to make sure nothing obscene, vulgar, or offensive ends up on a vanity plate. But with a little ingenuity, luck, and an inattentive or dim-witted beaurocrat (plenty of those to go around), sometimes one slips through! Check out these examples.

WASHIT

FISHIT

Johnny McCoy gets away with a "fishy" license plate. Check this out real close — wonder how it got by the DMV?

We're talking about fishing again. Yeah, right.

The Saga of Dennis Udink

Dennis Udink ran into a bureaucratic brick wall when he tried to get a license plate with his last name on it. The Utah DMV isn't budging despite his numerous appeals. His story made national news. Dennis thinks he's getting the shaft. After all, every Tom, Dick, and Harry can get their name put on a plate, but not him. (Come to think of it, Dick could get stiffed by the DMV too ...)

The DMV censors in Utah won't let Dennis Udink put his last name on a plate, yet Nevada had no problem issuing this one. Go figure. Dennis: Move to Nevada; problem solved!

Can Somebody Please Help This Man?

Jared Thompson, owner of Specialties Automotive Group, thinks about what should go on this Ferrari he has for sale. (Is [4RE] already taken?) Got any ideas for him?

When looking for that special vehicle, discriminating buyers know they can count on Jared for the best deal in the country. Check out his Web site (**www.SpecialtiesAuto.com**). You'll see what I mean.

Jose Gets a License Plate

One day my friend Jose wanted a personalized plate. So he went to the DMV with his application, and was told that his selection had already been taken. After several weeks Jose thought of another plate idea. He went back to the DMV and was told that plate combination had already been issued as well. Jose was very frustrated but finally came up with what he thought was the perfect plate—but no avail. He was told that too had already been taken. The DMV employee just looked at him and said: "I'm sorry. There's just no way, Jose. That one's taken, too."

Jose looked at her with surprise but knew he had his plate.

A few weeks later it was issued: NOAJOSE

The Family Car

There's nothing like a creative personalized plate to help promote family unity. Check out the family-themed plates on the next few pages.

Just exactly how many are there?

Houston, we've got a problem . . . the "mother load" has landed.

GMC

GOTKIDS

MOMMOBL

MOTHR·LD

Margo Ferrin poses with her load of kids and very clever license plate.

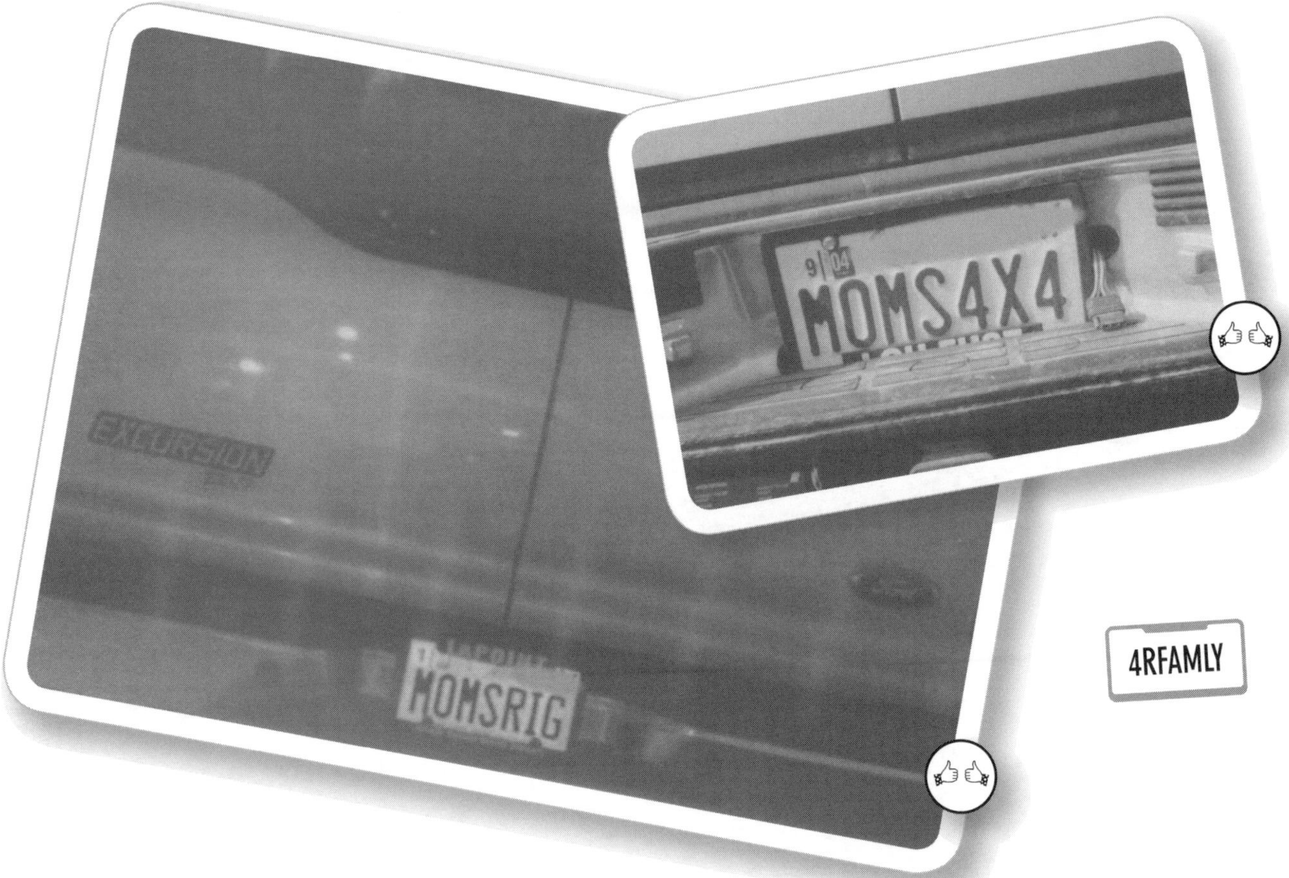

MOMS4X4

EXCURSION

MOMSRIG

4RFAMLY

Ah, the joys of big families!

8 HUGS

That's what it can seem like when the kids start howling "Are we there yet?" within the first 20 miles.

Rahae Dalgleish (nicknamed "Rae") poses with her son — the "kid" her plate is talking about. She must have had to do a lot of fast talking to get this one cleared!

THEMES

Girl Talk

Our boys have to ride in the Ford Explorer. This one's just for our girls!

The votes are in, guys. The girls have it.

You've heard of "My Three Sons"? Well, here are "my four girls"!

Proving once again that there's more
than one way to spell a phrase.
Isn't it interesting that neither of
these is on a Yugo?

The Grammies

Ladies and gentlemen, we now present to you . . .
the grammies!

What do you want to bet
her name is Susan?

So, which one's Grandma?

Fonny's personalized plate ain't the funniest plate I've ever seen, but it sure is the "fonniest"!

Bratty Plates

bein' a brat

BNABRAT

Meet Super Brat.

THEMES

Plates with Attitude

If attitude determines altitude, then these cars are flyin' low!

You want your car to have "attitude" too? See if you can come up with additional spellings.

| ATITUDE | ATTATUD | | ATTA2UD | ADDA2UD |

THEMES

Thanks for the warning.

Some Really "Bad" Plate Ideas

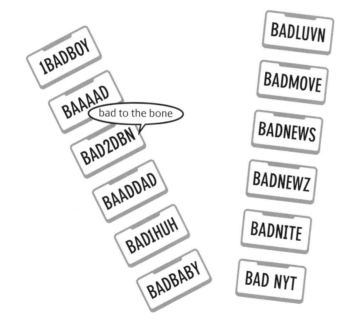

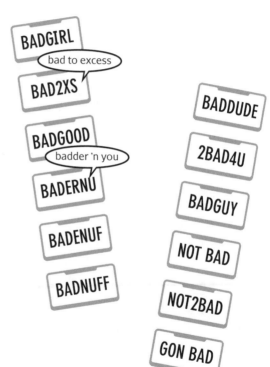

Nice Plates

Aren't these Nevada drivers nice?

Plates You Will "Like"

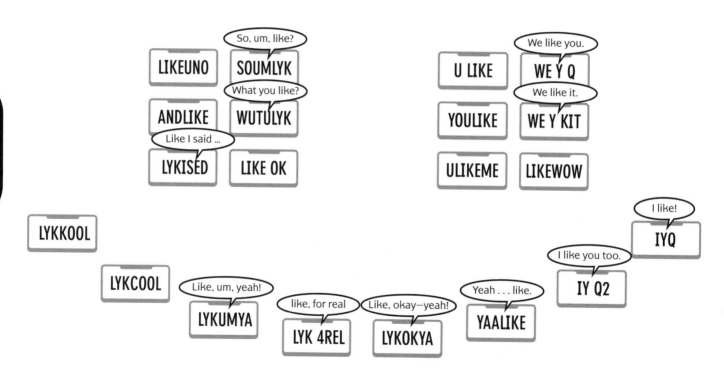

Are Personalized Plates Banned in Denver?

In the summer of 2002, I was in Denver for six days giving motivational seminars, and I never saw one personalized plate the entire time. Yet I've seen plenty of Colorado personalized plates on the freeways in other parts of the country. Are you Colorado personalized plate owners ashamed to be seen in your own state? It's time for you to step up to the "plate."

The Entertainment Section

I thought Letterman drove a Jeep Wrangler?

Beatlemania lives on!

Montana resident Brent Downey says this doesn't refer to a bottle of cheap wine, but to Jerry Garcia and the Grateful Dead. (Honk if you're a Dead Head!)

THEMES

Now what was that show? Saturday Night something or other? John ... um ... um ...

Trent Byers, Las Vegas bartender, has a plate that really rocks!

Are we talking about the rock band — or the driver?

THEMES

Kool PL8Z for Cool Cars

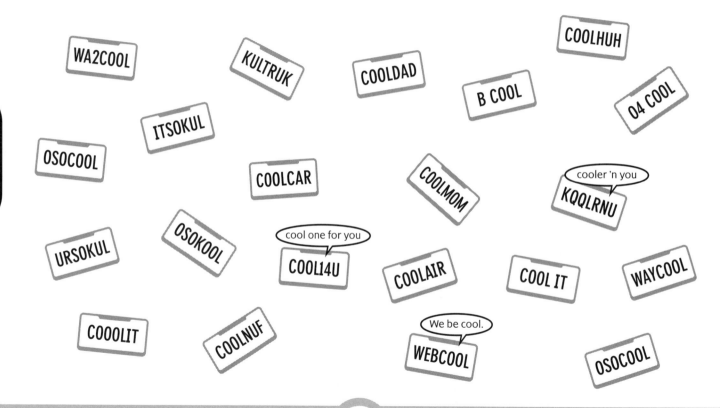

Dot-Com Mania

Many states allow a period, a comma, a dot, or an apostrophe. Typically, these characters are ignored in counting how many characters are on the plate. So, if your domain name is up to four characters long, you could fit the whole thing (minus either the "www." or the ".com") on your plate. Here are some examples.

IML8.COM	WWW.COM	.COMWTME	NOMO.COM
CU.COM	WOW.COM	.COMHERE	NODO.COM
HI.COM	FUN.COM	.COMTHIS	CRZ.COM

Got Gas?

When checking out fellow motorists' rear ends—that is, their autos' rear ends—what comes more readily to mind than gas? There's no shortage of gas-themed plates on the road, as these samples will attest. I thought these plates were a gas!

Hey, look!
A complete sentence in traffic:

Best stay 20 feet back!

Wanna Biggie-Size That?

Who says size doesn't matter? Okay, so you don't own a big piece of equipment. You can still drive your message home with a potent plate. Here are some size-themed plate ideas that should do the trick. When it comes time to order your plate from the DMV, just ask the friendly lady, "Can I biggie-size that for 39 cents?"

BIGYSYZ	BGGYSYZ	XXXLRG
BIGYSIZ	BGYSIZE	SUPRSYZ

Greg's big toy for a big boy.
Big man poses with his huge truck
and a fun plate.

THEMES

Seize the Day!

No matter how you say it—"*carpa diem*" or "seize the day"—plates like these are sure to grab other motorists' attention.

All those who saw Dead Poets' Society please honk your horn.

Take a Walk on the Wild Side!

Here are some wild ideas for your plate.

WILD14U

in the wild
ND WILD

WILD 1

wet 'n' wild
WTNWILD

WILDBCH

You see a wild one.
UCAYLD1

WLDTHNG

WILDQT

WILD QT

wild pony
WILDPNY

wild bunch
YLDBNCH

YLD QT

WILDWMN

too wild for you
2WILD4U

wet 'n' wild
WETNYLD

WILDRYD

BNWILD

born to be wild
BN2BYLD

RU2WILD

RUWILD

JS2WILD

WA2WILD

UAWILD1

jus' too wild
JS2YLD

THEMES

Cops and Robbers

Bad boys bad boys, who you gonna call?
Jackie Baum, (left) poses with daughter,
Tiphanie, and the author.

COPS is pretty gutsy, huh?

Jackie says cops love it!

Draggin' Main

How many ways can you say "My car's faster than yours" in seven characters or less?

Look both ways, check for flashing red lights, then …

NEVADA — GUN IT

NEVADA — RACR

Great economy of letters. This one could work on a motorcycle plate too.

NEVADA — SCREAMN

Crazy Plates

There are a lot of crazy drivers out there. If their driving doesn't convince you, just check out their plates.

Now taking reservations for the Bates Motel . . .

Look out! UPS pilot Kevin Bates (shown here with his son Troy) is really "psycho"!

psycho
CY CO

Gee, Dear, that sure looks like the Crazy family ahead. You remember Bill and Mary Crazy from the old neighborhood?

Don't say you haven't been warned.

Who would have ever imagined that a loony bin had wheels?

Warning Signs

The yellow signs off to the side aren't the only ones on the road. You'll spot them on the tail of passing cars too.

At least the guy's honest!

JEKYLL AND WHO?

Most cops have a hard time keeping a straight face when they pull up behind these plates!

We've got trouble . . . .

. . . and **major** trouble!

Busted! Carrie Christensen explains: "Uh-oh" is what her parents say every time she gets a traffic ticket.

Always the practical joker . . .

My apologies to whoever owns this plate. I shot this photo on the freeway one night. The flash startled the driver. (Probably thought a UFO was behind him!)

Attention law enforcement officers everywhere — she's "licensed" to be on the phone!

To all the Tara's in the world — here's your plate! (A plate is a terrible thing to waste.)

THEMES

Eight out of ten drivers say, "yeah, right," as they drive past without making eye contact.

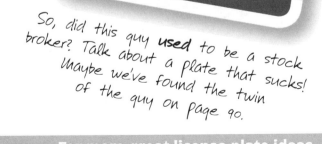

Careful, dear! Something tells me the driver up ahead is dangerous . . .

So, did this guy **used** to be a stock broker? Talk about a plate that sucks! Maybe we've found the twin of the guy on page 90.

Pessimists' Paradise

So, is the gas tank half full or half empty? I'll bet if we asked these guys, they'd say it was riddled with bullet holes and stuffed with sand.

This driver looks bummed out.

Does this refer to how they drive? Or how their last date was? Or the stupid movie they saw last weekend? Or the kinda fish he likes to catch? We need an explanation . . .

If you had a plate like this, you'd be grumpy too!

Was MIZRABL already taken?

Positively Positive Plates

Don't worry ...

now, let's all whistle the tune ...

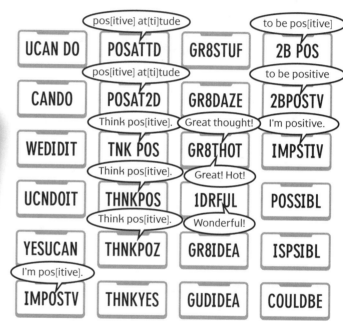

UCAN DO	POSATTD *pos[itive] at[ti]tude*	GR8STUF	2B POS *to be pos[itive]*
CANDO	POSAT2D *pos[itive] at[ti]tude*	GR8DAZE	2BPOSTV *to be positive*
WEDIDIT	TNK POS *Think pos[itive].*	GR8THOT *Great thought!*	IMPSTIV *I'm positive.*
UCNDOIT	THNKPOS *Think pos[itive].*	1DRFUL *Great! Hot!*	POSSIBL
YESUCAN	THNKPOZ *Think pos[itive].*	GR8IDEA *Wonderful!*	ISPSIBL
IMPOSTV *I'm pos[itive].*	THNKYES	GUDIDEA	COULDBE

ITHNKSO

If I am chosen as Miss Galaxy, I want to devote myself to …

WRL DPCE

But Dad, it could happen!

WAY POZ

Let's see, hmmmm, "Happy and Free": Either they just got out of a bad marriage or just signed up with a multi-level marketing company. I say 5 STARS!

NEVADA
ITCDHPN

POSBABE

U THINK

POSDUDE

I see you are AOK.
ICURAOK

UTHNKSO

RUPOSTV

THEMES

And to think only 50 vehicles in America will have this spelled exactly like this.

Real estate agent Mabel Murray-Moss (posing with her dog Muschci) believes in living life to the fullest.

Sure beats being in a rut!

Are you feeling lucky? Pam Dust says Bryan White's song inspired this plate.

Let the Good Times Roll

Lecia Johnson and Joyce Lewellyn are in it just for fun and they have fun getting noticed by anyone who comes across their path.

THEMES

THEMES

If you were stuck in jail in a banana republic and had only one phone call to make, Brad Eyre is the guy you'd want to call. He's a real-life Clint Eastwood, straight from a Dirty Harry movie.

After seeing this plate spelled a million different ways (XTAC, XTC, etc.), this driver confirms once again that we are NOT hooked on FONIX!

THEMES

What Are the Odds?

This really did happen, honest!

My friend and her daughter and I were leaving the parking lot of a movie theater in Sandy, Utah. Her daughter got all excited about something and exclaimed, "WOOHOO!"

And then I said, "Wouldn't it be funny if we saw 'Woohoo' on a license plate?"

No sooner did I get those words out of my mouth, than an SUV pulled out in front of us with the phrase "WOOHOOO" on the plate.

So whoever you are in that SUV in Utah, thanks for making our night!

Drive Time Religion

Some people wear their religion on their sleeve. Others prefer to wear it on their bumper.

"And the truth shall make you free!" Here are the facts: While in Las Vegas we met James and Carmen Clark and their new Mercedes. James tells me that he found this car on eBay for waaaaay less than any local dealers. He said that God had blessed them; hence the plate. They own Buena Vista Coffee Shop in Vegas. When in town, pay them a visit!

ALL4GOD

BELIEVE

ITSASIN

For those of you who missed Sunday school this week, shown here are four plates seen in a Target parking lot all at the same time! They must have just gotten out of church. Now they'll probably go over to Denny's for shakes. Think?

There's no mistakin' whose side this driver's on!

Heaven-bound too

THEMES

Midlife Crises

Okay. so you're having a midlife crisis. You've bought the car and the mistress. Now all you need to complete the picture is the plate! Here are some ideas.

I worked my tail off for 40 years, and all I get is this Jaguar?

THEMES

The Dirty Dozen

The following plates are **TABU** . Here are twelve license plates (or types of plates) you should never have on your car.

PAID 4	ALL MINE	SPOILED	MY VETT
DARRELL	DARREL1	U NV ME	IMTAKEN
BADR NU	RICHBCH	MRRIGHT	IMAHOTY

Let's make it a baker's dozen: **MORON**

A plate with your name on it is personalized, alright. Sure, it'll help you find your car in a Wal-Mart parking lot. But it lacks creativity. If you have to follow your name with a number, that's even worse. Then everyone knows that somebody else with the same name beat you to it! As a personalized plate owner, you have a civic duty to make your plate entertaining.

What's in a Name?

Putting your name on a personalized plate is okay as long as you do it creatively. Here are some good examples.

Does he want something, or did he win the car? No, his name is Michael Iwaniec.

This plate may not be as generic as it appears. What if the owners' names are Jennifer and Eric? You never know ...

THEMES

How many people could put their entire first and last name on a license plate — all five syllables — like Andy Anderson, here?

Rick West found a clever way to put his name on his plate.

Julio, you've done yourself proud!

Gregory Hyde turns a lot of heads with his creative plate. Just call him "Mister."

Is this another way of putting "Just Married" on the honeymoon getaway car?

At first you'd think this was the owner's name. Chelsea Watkins just wanted to create a name for her car. (Is that so wrong?)

A Credence fan is busted in traffic.

The Name Has Been Changed to Protect the Innocent

Did you hear about the guy who couldn't afford the personalized plate fee?

He changed his name to 015 LHB.

(Note: something like this appeared in the movie *Fargo*.)

Plate Violation Dismissed!

Meet Cyndi Gilbert—attorney, land developer, Harley lady, and cowgirl. When you're married to someone like construction magnate Steve Gilbert, you can get away with just putting your initials on the back of your Mercedes SL 550! Cyndi is a high-energy, make-it-happen person. Maybe for her next plate she could order GO GETTR .

Who's Your Daddy?

Successful real estate agent Ned Chidester likes to remind his kids who their father is.

So . . . who's **your** daddy?

Got Time for a QWIKEE?

If you need a quickie, here are a few ideas for you:

4AQWIKY	OSMQWKY *(awesome quickie)*	QWKYWOW	AH KWIKY
QWKYTYM *(quickie time)*	QWKY OK	1MOQWKY *(one more quickie)*	HEYQWKY
MYQWIKY	QWIKCHC	QWKYPLZ *(Quickie, please!)*	GOTQWKY
QWIKY4U	KWIKCHC	OSOQWIK	YORQWKY
KWIKY4U	KWIKFUN	OSOKWIK	YRQWIKY *(your quickie)*
SUMQWKY	RUAQWKY	MMMQWKY	N N OUT

Think fitting your message into just seven characters is tough? Try saying it in four or less on a motorcycle plate! Paul Stoddard has done a great job here.

THEMES

The ABCs of Traffic Talk

You've always wanted to learn a second language. Here's one you can learn in just a few minutes. It's called "Traffic Talk"—the language used to communicate on license plates. With this introduction and the examples throughout this book, you can master this language with just a few short weeks of practice!

The nice thing about Traffic Talk is that there are no big words. They can't be any longer than seven characters—including spaces in most cases. But you can usually slip in a small extra character like a dot or an apostrophe. Check with your state's DMV.

Many things you can say in English just can't be said in Traffic Talk, even if the DMV censors will let you, but you'll be amazed just how much **can** be translated into Traffic Talk using these simple approaches:

Abbreviate It. Unstressed and short vowels can usually be omitted safely, but be careful about removing long vowels. A short vowel in front of an **R** can almost always be eliminated.

EXAMPLES: RGETAWY = our getaway; FACELFT = facelift; HOMSELR = home seller; INSTMSG = instant message; COUNSLR = counselor

Misspell It. Especially if the character combination you want is already taken, substitute characters with their phonetic equivalents. **S** can often be exchanged with **C** or **Z**, and vice versa. **C, K,** or even **Q** can replace **CK** or the **K** sound. A slight misspelling actually adds to the comic effect.

EXAMPLES: LUVROX = love rocks; NEWZGUY = news guy; JUS2QIK = just too quick

Spell It Phonetically. This is an extension of the previous approach. Instead of replacing a character or two, think in terms of alternate ways the word or phrase could be spelled and still be pronounced the same.

EXAMPLES: OSM = awesome; BCNEWE = be seein' you; SEAULTR = see you later; WA UPHI = way up high

Use the Name of the Letter or Number. The names of several letters and numbers form the phonetic equivalent of words, syllables, or sounds.

EXAMPLES: GR8 = great; Y = why; 2DIE4 = to die for; 01812 = oh, I ate one too; REALST8 = real estate; CMEB4DK = see me before decay; 24TNT42 = two for tea and tea for two

Use Phonetic Abbreviations. There are several combinations of letters or numbers whose names, when pronounced together, can be very handy in replacing multiple syllables or words.

EXAMPLES: EZ = easy; NRG = energy; QT = cutie; RUA = are you a; IM = I am; UCA = you see a; N2 = into; YRU = why are you

Mispronounce It. Sometimes something that can't be translated into Traffic Talk when pronounced correctly, can be with a slight mispronunciation. This can also come in handy when what you want is already taken. And, like misspelling, it adds to the humor.

EXAMPLES: WSSUP = what's up; I EAR U = I hear you; SUHWEET = sweet; IMDBOSS = I am the boss

Use Character Puns. Usually this involves multiple copies of a character.

EXAMPLES: IRIGHTI = right between the eyes; NMY TTTT = in my forties; SNAKE II = snake eyes; IM YY4U = I'm too wise for you; XQQME = excuse me

Use Traffic Talk Conventions. Become acquainted with the handful of common abbreviations used on license plates.

EXAMPLES: D = the; BB = baby; LV = love; M = am, I'm; T = the, to; YA = yeah; Z = the

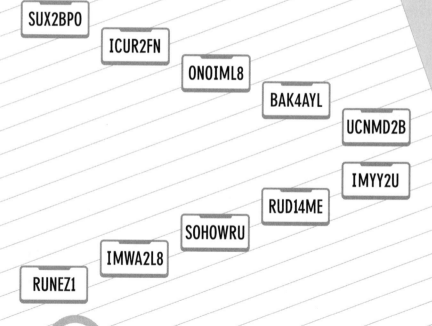

Where Do You Draw the Line?

Let's see how well you have mastered the language of Traffic Talk so far. On the left is a list of phrases; on the right are a bunch of license plates. Connect each phrase to its translation into Traffic Talk.

1. Are you the one for me?
2. So, how are you?
3. I am way too late.
4. I'm wise to you.
5. You see an MD to be.
6. Are you an easy one?
7. Oh no, I'm late!
8. Sucks to be poor
9. Back for awhile
10. I see you are too fun.

SUX2BPO

ICUR2FN

ONOIML8

BAK4AYL

UCNMD2B

IMYY2U

RUD14ME

SOHOWRU

IMWA2L8

RUNEZ1

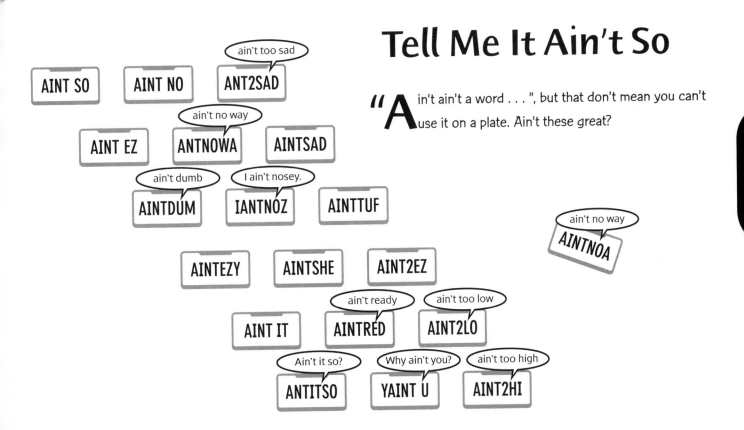

Tell Me It Ain't So

"**A**in't ain't a word . . . ", but that don't mean you can't use it on a plate. Ain't these great?

The "B" Attitudes

ABCs

BUD WHO

Be straight.
BE STR8

BE TRUE | **BUCKLUP** | **BETSOFF**

Back off!
BAAKOFF | **BE NICE** | **BOO HOO** | **BPLAYFL** | *breezin' by you* **BRZNBYU** | **BUT MOM** | *born to rock* **BRN2ROC** | **BEECOOL**

BAKTALK | **BOUTNEW** | **BOOWHO** | **BPLAFUL** | **BUCKYOU** | **B STILL** | *born to rock* **BRN2ROK** | **BEKOOL**

been busy
BNBUSY | **BOTMSUP** | *Banzai!* **BON ZI** | *Be wonderful.* **B1 DRFL** | **BUMDARN** | **B PALS** | *born to rock* **BRN2ROQ** | **UBECOOL**

Bottoms up! | *born too late* | *busy tonight?* | *broke now* | *born crazy*
BPOLITE | **BOTMZUP** | **BORN2L8** | **BPOSTIV** | **BSY2NYT** | **BSECURE** | **BROKNOW** | **BRNCRZY**

Be pleasant. | *bottom line* | *born to love* | | | | | *buff and tough*
BPLEZNT | **BTMLINE** | **BRN2LUV** | **BPOSITV** | **BUSTYOU** | **BE SAFE** | **BROKEME** | **BUFNTUF**

born to excel | *bright eyes* | | | | *buffin' it*
BEPERKY | **BOOTY4U** | **BORN2XL** | **BRYTIZE** | **BUT DAD** | **BSERIOS** | **BE COOL** | **BUFFNIT**

BOOHISS	BSUMFUN	BULWNKL	BUSHIT	BUTGOOD	BUTYFUL	BMPULSV
						Be impulsive.
BSTWIFE	BSOMFUN	BULSHIP	BUSHIS1	BUTHUNY	BUSYGUY	BMPLSIV
best wife						
BEST YF	B SQUARE	BUMSHOT	BUSYBDY	BTHONEY	BZYBUNY	B4 REEL
Be somebody.				*butterfly*		
BSUMBDY	B FLAT	BUMCRZY	BZ BODY	BUTAFLY	BZYGURL	BEMYFUN
					Be on time.	
BSUMONE	BSPUNKY	BUMWHAT	BUSYONE	BUT I DO	BONTIME	BZYMAMA
Be someone.		*bunny wabbit*				
B SUM 1	BSLOWER	BUNIWBT	BUSY 1	BUTWEET	BULLONY	B QUIET
		Be intuitive.				
BUTWEAT	BE HOME	BN2ITIV	BZYBEES	BZYGIRL	BUGSUM1	B4 REAL
		Be one to care.				
BUKWEAT	BIGTIME	B12CARE	BZYBEEZ	BUMDOUT	BUMLEGS	BUCWEAT

ABCs

Baby Your Baby

For a lot of people, their car is their "baby." So why not "pamper" your "baby" with a plate like these?

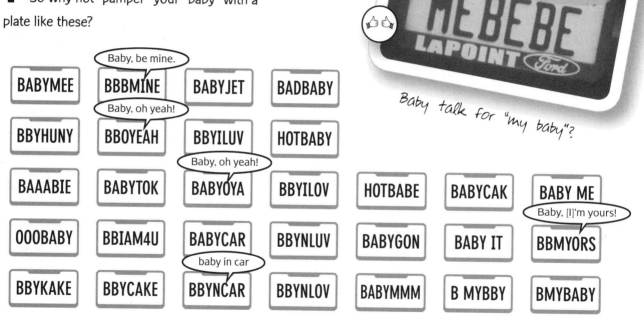

Baby talk for "my baby"?

BABYMEE	BBBMINE (Baby, be mine.)	BABYJET	BADBABY
BBYHUNY	BBOYEAH (Baby, oh yeah!)	BBYILUV	HOTBABY

BAAABIE	BABYTOK	BABYOYA (Baby, oh yeah!)	BBYILOV	HOTBABE	BABYCAK	BABY ME
OOOBABY	BBIAM4U	BABYCAR	BBYNLUV	BABYGON	BABY IT	BBMYORS (Baby, [I]'m yours!)
BBYKAKE	BBYCAKE	BBYNCAR (baby in car)	BBYNLOV	BABYMMM	B MYBBY	BMYBABY

ABCs

BBYTWUK · BABY4U · OBABYNO · BBYDUX · BABYDOL · OBABYAA · UMYBABY

BBYTALK · BBYDOLL · BABYICU · BBYIML8 · HI BBY · CYABABY

The I's Have It

But wait 'til next year's body change! Then you're in trouble!

I love cuties.
ILUVQTZ

I love cuties.

ILONG4U

I love cuties.
ILOVQTZ

I like it.
IWIKETT

ILUST4U

ILUVMOM

I doubt it.
IDOUTIT

I looked for you.
ILUKD4U

ILOVSNO

ILOOK4U

ILVLUCY

ILIKEIT

ILQQK4U

ILVSUMR

I like it.
ILYK IT

ILOVEU

I love cuties.
ILUVQTZ

I like it.
I Y KIT

ILVSUMR

The Big "O"

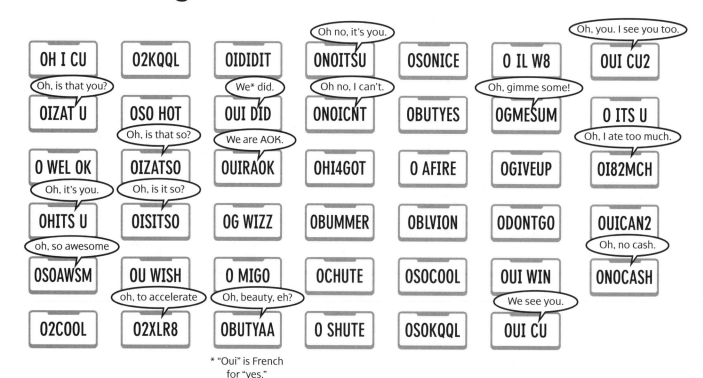

OH I CU

Oh, is that you?
OIZAT U

O WEL OK

Oh, it's you.
OHITS U

oh, so awesome
OSOAWSM

O2COOL

O2KQQL

OSO HOT

Oh, is that so?
OIZATSO

Oh, is it so?
OISITSO

OU WISH

oh, to accelerate
O2XLR8

OIDIDIT

We* did.
OUI DID

We are AOK.
OUIRAOK

OG WIZZ

O MIGO

Oh, beauty, eh?
OBUTYAA

Oh no, it's you.
ONOITSU

Oh no, I can't.
ONOICNT

OHI4GOT

OBUMMER

OCHUTE

O SHUTE

OSONICE

OBUTYES

O AFIRE

OBLVION

OSOCOOL

OSOKQQL

O IL W8

Oh, gimme some!
OGMESUM

OGIVEUP

ODONTGO

We see you.
OUI WIN

OUI CU

Oh, you. I see you too.
OUI CU2

O ITS U

Oh, I ate too much.
OI82MCH

OUICAN2

Oh, no cash.
ONOCASH

* "Oui" is French
for "yes."

ABCs

The "What"s District

There must be fifty ways to ask the eternal question, "What's up?" Here are a few.

[What]'s up, baby?
SUP BB

WAASSUP

[What]'s up, man?
SUP MAN

WSOPMAN

WSUPMAN

OK WSUP

Oh, gee, what's up?
OGWSSUP

MANWSUP

Like, what's up?
So, man, what's up?

HEYWSUP

LYKWSUP

SMNWSUP

Yeah, what's up?
I know what's up.

YAWSSUP

INOWSUP

WHATSUP

You know what's up.

WASSSUP

UNOWSUP

WAHSSUP

Hey, so what's up?
Come on, [what]'s up?

WZUPDOC

HASWSUP

CMONSUP

Whatever is up, I'm up for it!

Doing a "Background Check"

Designer plates are all the rage nowadays. I'm talking about the fancy backgrounds that the states print on the plates. Some have scenic backgrounds; others are customized for special events or particular occupations, hobbies, or interests. When you go in to the DMV to order your personalized plate, you may be tempted to spring for one of these fancy plates while you're in the mood to spend extra money. But before you do, a "background check" may be in order. Often the fancy backgrounds make the characters difficult to read. You want your message to be read, don't you? Don't let it be obscured by a bunch of other stuff. If your state still offers an old-fashioned, plain white background, go for that. Then you can be sure that people will be able to read your plate. As if it isn't hard enough to come up with a good plate idea that isn't already taken, some states are still fixated on using some of the characters to identify the county. Or they think it's cute to throw in a bucking horse or a state outline, a fruit, or some other emblem between the characters, making your job all the tougher. Often you are left with only four characters to work with. If you live in one of those states, I feel your pain. Good luck! Maybe it's time to lobby your legislature.

AKA HOT	AKAGOOD	AKAHULK	AKAKRAZ
AKACOOL	AKABEMR	AKA FUN	AKAKRZY
AKA ACE	AKABIMR	AKAFUN1	AKACRZY
AKABOZO	AKAFAST	AKAKOOL	AKAVDUB
AKABIG1	AKAFOXY	AKAKQQL	AKABABE
AKA BAD	AKA JOE	AKAKILR	AKABABY
AKABAYB	AKABUNZ	AKA L8R	AKABYBY
AKA BB	AKAIML8	AKAGONE	AKADUH
AKAALSO	AKABUNS	AKA CYA	

Traveling with an Assumed Name

Ever notice the strange little abbreviation, "aka"? It stands for "also known as . . ." and is used to indicate aliases or assumed names. You can put it to clever use on your plate.

> Just call me Dad.

AKAPAPA

Who's your daddy?

Busy Signals

Are you too busy to take the time to spell things out? Well, heck, you can even abbreviate "busy." Check out these impatient plates.

BUSYNOW

IM2BZ4U

BUSYL8R

BUSYBEE

U BUSY

WA2BUZY

HOWBZRU

BZ2NITE

ABZYGUY

UBZ2NYT

ABZYGAL

BUSYHUH

ICUR BZ

OUBZNOW

ABZYGRL

BUSYDUH

WA2BUSY

IMBZDUH

UBZ L8R

UBZ BEE

CU IMBZ

MY URBZ

F itting the word "easy" on a plate is easy when you abbreviate it "EZ".

EZ Does It

EZ MONY	EZ2PLEZ	EZ WERK	EZ2BEME	ITSNTEZ	EZ HUH	EZ2KUDL	EZTRUKN
EZMONEY	EZBABY	TAKIT EZ	EZ RYDR	EZ4U2NO	EZ DUH	EZ2KISS	EZWAYS
EZ MUNY	EZON ME	EZ HOT E	EZRIDER	EZ4U2SA	EZ BABY	KISMEEZ	EZ 1HUH
EZ CASH	GO EZ	EZ4ME2B	ITS EZ	EZ PKUP	EZGOING	EZ4SURE	LIKE2EZ
EZ 2 LUV	GO EZ OK	EZ DO IT	ITSEASY	EZHOTTY	EZ GOIN	EZBLOND	EZDO ME
EZ2LOVE	EZ WORK	EZ DZIT	O ITS EZ	2EZ4ME	EZ2CUDL	EZREDHD	EZRNL

easy to cuddle (EZ2KUDL)

easy to cuddle (EZ2CUDL)

easy redhead (EZREDHD)

easier [tha]n hell (EZRNL)

The Great IM

The abbreviation "IM" is a popular and easily understood space saver for "I am".

IMCRAZY

IMKRAZY

IMKRA Z

IMGOING

IMGOIN

IM GONE

I'm a believer.
IMABLVR

IMANURS

IMANERD

IMAPLYR

I'm a mommy.
IMAMOMY

I'm a daddy.
IMADADY

IMFUNRU

I'm bonkers.
IMBNKRS

I'm in denial.
IMNDNYL

I'm hatin' it.
IMH8NIT

I'm so poor.
IMSO PO

I'm in rehab.
IMNREHB

IMNOLDY

IMNACE

IM 1 RU

I'm in for fun.
IMN4FUN

IMN2FUN

IMATOY

IMFUNRU

I'm a cutie.

IMA QT

IM1 RU2

IM LOST

IM2GOOD

I'm in trouble.

IMNTRBL

I'm in too deep.

IMN2DP

IMNLOVE

IMNLOV2

IMNLUV2

IMNUTS

IMNUTZ

I'm a lover.

IMALUVR

I'm a fighter.

IMAFYTR

. . . but I've got an "innie" — does that count?

IM-LEFTY

Getting N2 It

The combination "N2" makes a handy substitute for "into."

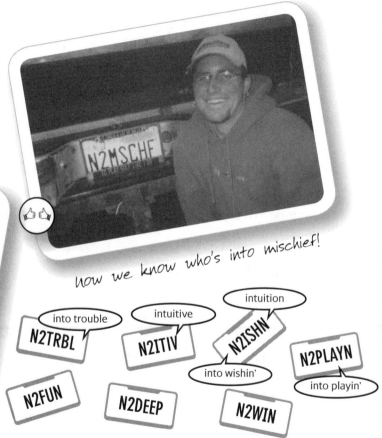

now we know who's into mischief!

A fitness buff? A repeat divorcé? An abrupt negotiator?

N2TRBL — into trouble
N2ITIV — intuitive
N2ISHN — intuition
N2PLAYN — into playin'
N2FUN
N2DEEP
N2WIN — into wishin'

The Energy Department

The combination "NRG" makes a great substitute for "energy". When it comes to personalized plates there's no creative energy shortage.

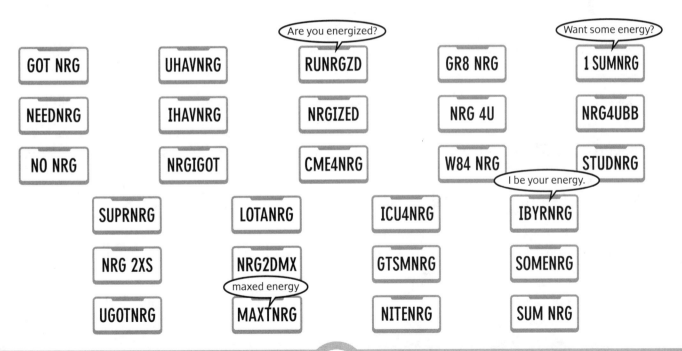

These Plates Are Just OK

Oklahoma may be the only state that is just "OK," but there are plenty of other "OK" plates out there on the road.

OK FINE	OK IOU	OK42DAY	OKICUBB	OKYDOKY	OK HUH	OK 4NOW	OK4ONCE
OK4A YL	OK UWIN	OK42NYT	OKSMILE	OK2BE U	OK DUH	OKITLDO	OKOKOK
OK DOIT	OK2 HUG	OKLEZGO	OK NOMO	OKIWILL	DUH UOK	OK2 EAT	OKIMGON
OK UNME	OKWHYME	OK ILCU	OKIOU2	OK FINE	OKYDOKY	OKIBCNU	I OK UOK
OK1MORE	OK Y ME	OKILCYA	OK BYBY	IMOK RU	ULOOKOK	OK BCN U	OKL8R YA
OK YALL	OK123GO	OKCYABY				OKIWONT	OKYA L8R

- OKICUBB — Okay, I see you, baby.
- OK4A YL — okay for a while
- OK NOMO — okay no more
- OKIBCNU — Okay, I be seein' you.
- OK Y ME — Okay, why me?
- OKL8R YA — Okay. Later. Yeah.
- OKCYABY — Okay. See ya. Bye!

Totally Awesome Plates

Wouldn't it be awesome if you could put "AWESOME" on your tag? Chances are, it's already taken in your state. But never fear: Here are some totally awesome ways to abbreviate it.

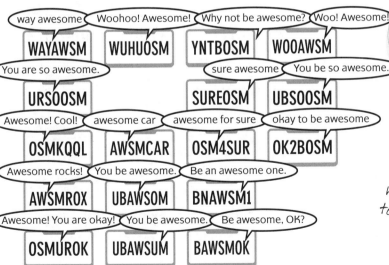

way awesome	Woohoo! Awesome!	Why not be awesome?	Woo! Awesome!
WAYAWSM	**WUHUOSM**	**YNTBOSM**	**WOOAWSM**

You are so awesome.		sure awesome	You be so awesome.
URSOOSM		**SUREOSM**	**UBSOOSM**

Awesome! Cool!	awesome car	awesome for sure	okay to be awesome
OSMKQQL	**AWSMCAR**	**OSM4SUR**	**OK2BOSM**

Awesome rocks!	You be awesome.	Be an awesome one.
AWSMROX	**UBAWSOM**	**BNAWSM1**

Awesome! You are okay!	You be awesome.	Be awesome, OK?
OSMUROK	**UBAWSUM**	**BAWSMOK**

Say "totally awesome," and anyone in the intermountain west automatically thinks of computer marketing genius Dell Schanze. "Super Dell," as he is known, told me this is the plate he would like to have. The DMV may not let him have it, but Photoshop did!

Cute Plates

The car may be cute; your plate idea may be cute too. But what if you have too much on your plate (excuse the pun) to fit "CUTE" or "CUTIE"? Never fear, there are "cute" abbreviations for just such situations.

What could be cuter than a Bug?

QT PIE	KEY UTE	MYQTBBY (my cutie baby)
CUTEYPI	QT AHED	BBURAQT (Baby, you are a cutie!)
ICUQTPI	URSOQUT (You are so cute.)	QT42NYT (cutie for tonight)
BMYQTPI	KQQL QT	ILBYRQT (I'll be your cutie.)
04 CUTE	OQT ICU (Oh cutie, I see you.)	BMYQTOK (Be my cutie, okay?)
CUTEHUH	BABY QT	NETYMQT (Any time, cutie.)

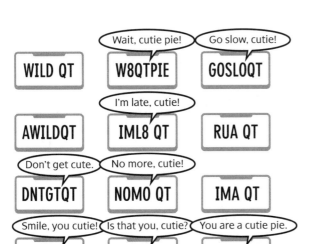

WILD QT

Wait, cutie pie! — W8QTPIE

Go slow, cutie! — GOSLOQT

AWILDQT

I'm late, cutie! — IML8 QT

RUA QT

Don't get cute. — DNTGTQT

No more, cutie! — NOMO QT

IMA QT

Smile, you cutie! — SMYLUQT

Is that you, cutie? — ZATU QT

You are a cutie pie. — URAQTPI

CUTESUV

MMMCUTE

LOOK QT

CUTENUF

FAST QT

Never mind the car. What about the gal inside?

tag tales

Montana:
License Plate Nirvana

Are personalized plates free in Montana or awfully inexpensive?

Once when I was going to give a motivational talk up in Bozeman, Montana, I stopped off in Butte for a few hours. I went down to visit the local newspaper on the main street and I couldn't believe my eyes. I counted eighteen vehicles with personalized plates in one city block.

RU What?!

Want to strike up a conversation in traffic? Try replacing "Are you . . . " with the magic combo "RU" on your plate.

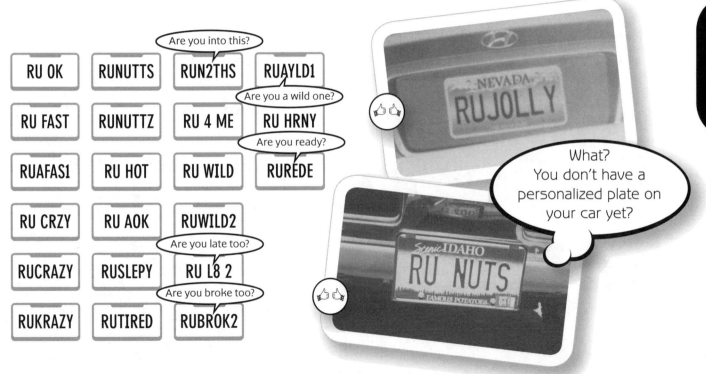

RU OK

RUNUTTS

RUN2THS — *Are you into this?*

RUAYLD1 — *Are you a wild one?*

RU FAST

RUNUTTZ

RU 4 ME

RU HRNY

RUAFAS1

RU HOT

RU WILD — *Are you ready?*

RUREDE

RU CRZY

RU AOK

RUWILD2

RUCRAZY

RUSLEPY

RU L8 2 — *Are you late too?*

RUKRAZY

RUTIRED

RUBROK2 — *Are you broke too?*

NEVADA — RUJOLLY

Scenic IDAHO — RU NUTS — FAMOUS POTATOES

What? You don't have a personalized plate on your car yet?

ABBREVIATIONS

RU a Teaser?

Here are some good teasers . . .

I'm just teasin'. IMJSTZN	*I'm not teasin'.* IMNTEZN	ILLTEZU
YUTEZME	1TEASER	Q TEASE
TEZE ME	TEASEME	ME A TEZ
URATEEZ	*Please tease.* PLEZTEZ	RUATEEZ
What a tease! WUTATEZ	*chick teaser* CHICTZR	ITEEZU
Don't tease me. DNTEZME	*I'm no tease.* IMNOTEZ	*I teased you.* ITEEZDU
	I'm not easy.	

ABBREVIATIONS

Well, XQZZZZ Me!

Driving around, you're sure to tick somebody off, even if you don't mean to. Wouldn't it be nice to have a plate like these to help smooth things over? There are plenty of ways to say "excuse me." I guess we could call these plates road rage insurance.

EXCUZME	MYEXCUZ	XQZZZME	NOEXCUZ
WLXQZME	NOXCUZE	XQZA ME	YORXCUZ
XCUZMOI	XQQQZME	SOXQZME	YERXQZD

Dr. Ted's 6-Step Recovery Program for Personalized Plate Addicts

STEP 1
Recognize and admit that you have been addicted to reading personalized license plates for most of your life.

STEP 2
Confess in front of two or more witnesses that certain license plates have caused excessive brain cramp when you have failed to figure out the message.

STEP 3
Have faith in a higher power that this book you are now holding is your answer to becoming a license plate reading expert.

STEP 4
Embrace the fact that even though all ordinary standard-issue license plates are actually personalized (because each is unique), having one on your car tells the world that you are boring.

STEP **5** With the enlightenment and inspiration you've received from this book, muster the strength and courage to open your creative mind and choose your own fun personalized license plate —the one you've always wanted.

STEP **6** Commit the 55 bucks (or whatever it costs in your state) to obtain your special plate and let drivers everywhere know that you are a fun, free-thinking, creative person and have tapped your imaginative powers, proving you are unafraid to stand out in the crowd!

Now, this takes guts!

Un-4GET-able Plates

UH OH	4GETU	IFORGOT	OGZI4GT
OI4 GOT	4GETYOU	4GOT2GO	4GVN4GT
I4GOT 2	IL4GTU2	I4GETEZ	4GET IT
DIDU4GT	O4GETIT	DONT4GT	
ME 4GET	JS4GET	ONOI4GT	
JU4GET	DNT4GET	O GEEZ	

Oh geez, I forgot! → OGZI4GT

Forgive and forget. → 4GVN4GT

I'll forget you too. → IL4GTU2

I forget easy. → I4GETEZ

Did you forget? → DIDU4GT

Jus' forget. → JS4GET

Oh no, I forgot! → ONOI4GT

[Di]d you forget? → JU4GET

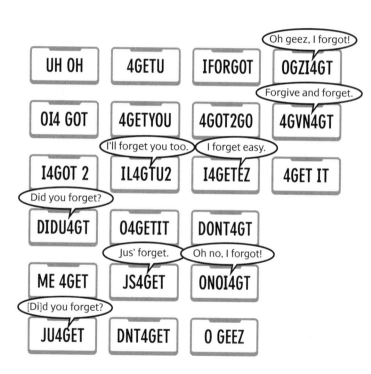

Dressed for Success

Many people buy an expensive car to show (or at least give the impression) that they are successful. Why not complete the picture with a "successful" plate? Just as "6E" makes a concise substitute for "SEXY", "6S" can replace "SUCCESS". Here are some examples.

ABBREVIATIONS

6SFUL	SIXSFUL	WISHU6S	6SFOOL	NO6SYET
6S FULL	6 SESS	6S 2U	DRES46S	NO6S4ME
RU6SFUL	6 CESS	NO 6S	6S SUX	

Crazy Eights

The numeral 8 is extremely handy. It can stand for "ate"; or, stick it with another character, and you can get "weight," "wait," "date," "bait," "mate," "fate," "date," etc.

H8 2 W8	SHES2L8	ICANTW8	OUT 2L8	W84MEOK — *Wait for me, okay?*
ITLL W8	SHEZ2L8	IWONTW8	L8 NITE	WEW84U — *We wait for you.*

Why not be late? YNOTBL8

now, here's a tempting PL8 F8 that's !

UJUS W8 — *You just wait!*	IM 2 L8	IDONTW8	L8NIGHT	W8N 2GO

I82MUCH

I'm late. So what? ML8SWUT

IH82W8 — *I hate to wait.*	ONOIML8	GONABL8	SRYIML8 — *Sorry I'm late.*	W8N4HER	MUSTBF8	ALWAZL8 — *always late*	L84WERK	GETTNL8

HES 2L8	PLEZ W8	MGNABL8 — *[I']m gonna be late.*	MANRUL8 — *Man, are you late!*	WELLW8	BOYRUL8	L8RT8R	NO4NK8N — *no fornicatin'*	GETUPL8

HEZ 2L8	PLZW8OK — *Please wait, okay?*	UGNABL8 — *You gonna be late.*	WILLUW8	SOOIML8	L8AGAIN	L8RTATR — *Later, tater.*	WRKNL8	GOTUPL8

Put Her in Reverse!

Plates in the mirror may be funnier than they appear. If a plate just doesn't seem to make sense, or if you want a better shot at slipping your plate idea under the censors' radar, consider how it may read in the mirror. Some characters (A, H, I, M, O, T, U, V, W, X, Y, 0, 1, 8) read the same both directions. But some can be read as a different character in the mirror. E and 3 become interchangeable. So do S or 5 and Z or 2. Or you can simply spell the word with the characters in reverse order. Dyslexic drivers should catch your drift, no problem!

ZUX3L

The perfect plate for the dyslexic Lexus driver.

DON'T GET IT?
11 04
YENSID
READ ME BACKWARDS

Don't get this one? When all else fails, follow the instructions.

license plate  test

Analyze This!

The license plates shown here are considered to be some of the most challenging plates on the American road. Some of them have been known to cause accidents by distracting the driver's attention and inciting serious arguments as a result.

Consider yourself an amateur if you can guess the meaning of only three or less.

Call yourself a License Plate Rookie if you can figure up to seven.

From there up to ten, you are in the top ten percent of license plate readers in the USA.

You are a Certified Professional License Plate Reader if you correctly answer all twelve in less than 90 seconds.

| IRIGHTI | NEDKCME | MYYFSSC | PONOMO | IMYY4U | YRWENLA |
| NETYMQT | UVBNXX | NE1410S | HIOFICR | K9GONIT | H2OUUP2 |

ANSWERS:

IRIGHTI = "right between the eyes"
NEDKCME = "any decay, see me"
MYYFSSC = "My wife's sexy."
PONOMO = "poor no more"
IMYY4U = "I'm wise for you."
YRWENLA = "Why are we in L.A.?"
NETYMQT = "Any time, cutie."
UVBNXX = "You've been double-crossed."
NE1410S = "Anyone for tennis?"
HIOFICR = "Hi, officer!"
K9GONIT = "Doggone it!"
H2OUUP2 = "What are you up to?"

Did I Say That?

Sometimes a standard-issue plate will look deceptively like a personalized plate. Look around—you might stumble on an inadvertently hilarious plate!

Lies! Lies! It's all a pack of lies!

Was this lifted from James Bond's Mercedes? Can't help but wonder . . .

Hmmm . . . Jack Kennedy had quite a reputation as a womanizer. But can't you ladies let him rest in peace?

The Marines would be satisfied with just a few good ones. What do we have here? A nymphomaniac? Some incredible polyandrist? Awfully provocative for a standard-issue plate ...

How to Get the Perfect Plate for You

If you see a plate combination in this book that appeals to you, check with the DMV in your state to see if it's available. If the particular plate you want it is not available, then try adapting it using various suggestions outlined in this book, like adding a letter or number or adjusting the spelling. Be careful—you may get a "brain cramp" like I did writing this book!

You may be able to check online at your state's Division of Motor Vehicles. (In Utah, where I now live, it's at **www.DMV.Utah.gov.**) But a word to the wise: my experience has been that if you check online to see if the combo you want is available, your request will almost always be rejected because the computers can't read. You're better off going to the DMV in person or calling on the phone.

It's important to remember that vulgar or explicit messages will probably get refused. If your plate does accidentally pass the DMV's screeners and an officer of the law spots it, the fines can be serious—I've heard of up to $1000 fines!

Random Excess

Some of the most entertaining plates are one-of-a-kind, off-the-wall, wacky plates like the ones on the following pages.

Like you're going to put BIGBUNZ on your plate!

Calling all canines:
This is the car to chase!

Is this a cry for help?

I guess we could have called this page our airhead section . . .

Is Dagwood in the passenger seat?

It's comforting to know somebody on the road has got a clue.

BEYOND1

Just the sort of plate you would expect to see around Las Vegas.

You just had to do it, didn't you?

I'm takin' my marbles and I'm . . .

NOCANDO

THISLDO

"Oops, I did it again!" Deanna Campbell sports one of the most memorable plates I've seen. Four letters can put out quite a message, huh?

Maybe he's a Rogaine distributor.

Italians everywhere are wondering how this plate got past the vigilant, well trained DMV screeners!

The ultimate getaway car.

Kathy Lawrence says, "We meet at high noon, or get out of Dodge!" But wait—she's already out of Dodge. That's a Chevy Silverado!

A rather frightening plate, don't you think? Always check the frame for the "rest of the story."

ARE YOU SEEING RED?

pretty in pink

The strange thing is, this was on a **red** car. Maybe they're waiting for the paint job to fade.

No, that's not "Lady Nerd"; it's "Lady in Red." The car is bright red. So's the coat and the lipstick. This gal seems bent on making everyone see red!

Wait, let me guess: This driver used to live in California and got so used to driving around with this on his plate that he couldn't part with it? Am I close?

Another California refugee? Or maybe a former patient in the state mental hospital? Couldn't help wondering.

GN2MAUI

2 MAUI

MAUI4ME

HNYLULU

Better than a
postcard —
greetings from
Rudy and
Ardie Tanega
of Las Vegas.
P.S.: I hope your
daughter's recovery
went well!
-Ted

Took me a couple of seconds to get
this one too! "Hawaiian Island" —
wish I was there!

Buddy, you're a long way
from home!

And Just What Is the Meaning of This?

Sometimes when you're reading personalized plates, you'll come across one like this. It's obviously a personalized plate, but what does it mean? "Tom's Tickets"? "Tim's Tickets"? "TMS Tickets"? Who knows? On plates like these, the owner hasn't given the reader enough clues to guess the meaning. When you encounter plates like this, don't let them get to you. Remember: as with anything else, some people are aces at coming up with plate ideas, while others flunk out. If reasonably experienced plate readers can't figure out what your plate says within a few seconds, you've lost your audience—and wasted your $50!

No, we wouldn't be following Doris Day, would we?

Jenny Taylor has found a clever way to say "C'est la vie!"

MISCELLANY

Who needs rules?

Who **says** you can't find an honest lawyer?

This was spotted, appropriately enough, in front of a Blockbuster store.

This one's so good, I wonder what their first choice was.

A matching pair of plates from the same state. Jean Goesch (pronounced "Gosh") proudly displays her OMY·GOSH plate while Jenni Williams poses by OMYHECK. Can you guess which state these plates are from? The answer should be obvious . . .

Patience, my son . . .

It's the propeller that makes this one work.

Betcha this one made you chuckle!

Don't follow this guy.
He'll never steer you right!

GONE POSTAL!

Watch out!
Lee Laird is goin' postal.

Some would say this is excessive.
I would say it is 2D MAX .

A most excellent plate.

Now, there's one **sumooth** operator!

One word says it all.
How about this variation:

SAW WEET

Thank goodness psychologist
Nicole Hawkins' was available to analyze
her plate for us. It says "mental floss,"
a term taken from a
Jimmy Buffett song.

MISCELLANY

License Plates of the Rich and Famous

Utah Jazz basketball star (#47) Andrei Kirilenko sports his nickname. What a killer plate!

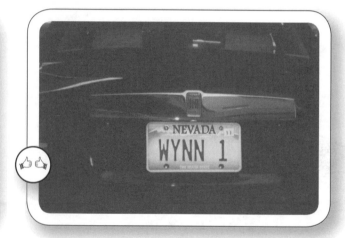

This gorgeous Rolls Royce belongs to Las Vegas casino magnate and billionaire Steve Wynn.

Final Exam

Now you are at the end of the book. It's time to put into practice everything you have learned. You have read hundreds of the most creative plates on the American road. You have been initiated to the secrets of the masters as to how to say what you want in seven characters or less. You have tested your skill at reading plates in the IQ tests throughout this book. But plate watching is not just a spectator sport. You want to get in the game yourself. You want to come up with the perfect creative plate for your car. So let's practice translating phrases into "traffic talk." Obviously, there are a lot of words and phrases that cannot be successfully reduced to seven characters or less. But all of these can. I guarantee it. Some can be done several ways. Let's see how you do! Fill in the plate to the right of the phrase.

Visit www.licenseplatefun.com to check your answers!

1. I am in too deep.

2. I want to tease you.

3. I can relate.

4. Where are you?

5. Be seein' you later

6. Are you way too busy?

7. Up too late for you

8. Hey, sexy baby!

9. I ate to excess.

Send in Your Sightings!

I hope you have enjoyed reading this book as much as I enjoyed putting it together. I have collected the funniest plates I could find, but with over ten million personalized plates out there, a few of them got away from me in traffic. If you've seen a plate or own one that you think should have been in this book, we'd like to hear from you! In fact, by going to **www.licenseplatefun.com** you can find out about our exciting contest (complete with prizes and giveaways) to discover the most clever and amusing license plates on the road. Who knows? Maybe your photo will make the cover of our next book! You'll find complete contest instructions, how to submit your photos, etc. by visiting our website: **www.licenseplatefun.com**. We'll see you online! Thanks for your help and interest. Creative plate owners rock!

To contact me directly, e-mail me at: ted@licenseplatefun.com